ISO 9000:2000 In a Nutshell

A Concise Guide to the Revisions

ISO 9000:2000
In a Nutshell

A Concise Guide to the Revisions

Jeanne Ketola
&
Kathy Roberts

Paton
Press

Chico, California

Most Paton Press books are available at quantity discounts when purchased in bulk. For more information, contact:

Paton Press
848 Rush Court
Chico, CA 95926
Telephone: (530) 342-5480
Fax: (530) 342-5471
E-mail: *books@patonpress.com*
Web: *www.patonpress.com*

ISBN 0-9650445-5-6

Staff
Publisher .... Scott M. Paton
Senior Editor .... Vanessa R. Franco
Assistant Editor .... Heidi M. Paton
Book Cover Design .... Edward C. Jones

Dedication

To Mom and Dad, who always said I could;
Chuck, Tim, Lida, and Jon, who inspire me every day;
My clients, who challenge themselves to be the best.
                                                        —Jeanne

To Ryan, who is my soulmate and best friend,
and to Austin, who is my pride and joy.
Thanks for reminding me what's important in life.
                                                        —Kathy

Contents

Chapter 1

Introduction

For many organizations, the upcoming revisions to the ISO 9000 family of standards will cause panic, shock, and confusion. For others, the transition from the old to the new will seem brief and relatively painless. The ease with which an organization adapts will depend largely on the maturity of its quality management system and the commitment of top management to continual improvement.

In the last year, much has been written about the revisions to the ISO 9000 series. As the revisions have passed each iteration on their path to becoming a released international standard, the public has had the opportunity to review the progress and comment on the drafts by means of a standardized template submitted to the American Society for Quality. Numerous Web sites are also available to help organizations with the changes. *(See Chapter 6 for a list of information sources on the new standards.)*

The consolidation of the ISO 9000 series will consist of the following four core documents, plus *ISO 10012 Measurement Control System* (a combination of *ISO 10012-1:1992 Metrological confirmation system for measuring equipment* and *ISO 10012-2:1997 Guideline for control of measurement processes*):

■ *ISO 9000:2000 Quality management systems—Fundamentals and vocabulary.* This document describes quality management system fundamentals and terminology. It cancels and replaces ISO 8402:1994 and ISO 9000-1:1994, clauses 4 and 5. *ISO 9000-1 Guidelines for the selection and use of the ISO 9000 series* has been published as a brochure by ISO.

■ *ISO 9001:2000 Quality management systems—Requirements.* This document defines the requirements for quality management systems and is used to demonstrate an organization's capability to provide products that meet customer and applicable regulatory requirements. It cancels and replaces

ISO 9001:1994, ISO 9002:1994, and ISO 9003:1994. Permissible exclusions, such as design, are allowed for those organizations that have used ISO 9002 and ISO 9003.

■ *ISO 9004:2000 Quality management systems—Guidelines for performance improvement.* This document provides guidance on quality management systems and includes concepts for continual improvement processes that link to customer satisfaction. It is intended to help organizations establish and improve their quality management systems, with an emphasis on performance improvement. It cancels and replaces ISO 9004-1:1994.

■ *ISO 19011 Guidelines on quality and environmental auditing.* This document provides guidance on managing and conducting quality and environmental audits and is intended to be a joint auditing document. It cancels and replaces ISO 10011 and is currently in the Committee Draft 1 (CD1) stage of development.

This book was written with the intent of presenting the revisions to ISO 9001 in a clear and concise manner. The book contains the specific information organizations need to know in order to understand the changes, communicate them to personnel at all levels, and implement the changes with minimal disruption to their systems. This book is unique in that it presents the changes in a format familiar to most organizations: the ISO 9001:2000 revisions are integrated within the 4.1–4.20 structure from the 1994 version. It should be noted, however, that this book is based on the Draft International Standard (DIS). Although we're confident that the DIS is representative of the final released standard, some changes may occur before final publication. Nevertheless, the information presented in this book will enable organizations to bring their current quality systems to ISO 9001:2000 compliance.

Because ISO 9001:2000 is based on a process management approach, the next chapter of this book focuses on this concept. Chapter 3 compares ISO 9001:2000's "new" requirements to those in the 1994 version. Chapter 4 examines some of the more noteworthy changes to ISO 9001. Chapter 5 offers tips on how to transition from ISO 9001:1994 to ISO 9001:2000. Chapter 6 addresses common concerns that organizations may have and contains a list of resources for more information.

As active members of the U.S. Technical Advisory Group (TAG) to ISO Technical Committee 176 (TC 176), we participate in discussions within Task Group 18. This group is responsible for evaluating the revisions to ISO 9001 and ISO 9004, generating a list of concerns, and developing the U.S. positions on these two standards. The U.S. delegates present these positions at the international meetings. Because we have been active members for more than six years, we have an in-depth knowledge of the standards-development process and possess first-hand information about the details of the revisions.

In addition to our participation in the U.S. TAG, we own successful management consulting practices specializing in ISO 9000 system implementation. We both have solid backgrounds in management and have worked in a variety of industries. Because we work with all levels of personnel from executive management to line employees, we have an inside view of ISO 9000 implementation. As such, we're able to understand top management's concerns regarding the revisions.

Our intent in writing this book was to provide those responsible for implementing and maintaining ISO 9001:2000 with a simple approach for understanding the revisions, as well as to answer the major questions they may have. We hope that this publication will become a well-used handbook during the change process.

In a nutshell, good luck and happy reading!

Chapter 2

Process Management

One of the first things you'll notice about ISO 9001:2000 is its new structure. The sections are no longer listed as 4.1–4.20, as they were in the 1994 version. ISO 9001:1994 was organized from a functional point of view. As a result, many organizations didn't link their processes together to build a management system. Instead, they organized it by specific areas of responsibility. For example, using ISO 9001:1994 as a basis, engineering would take responsibility for 4.4 Design Control, customer service would take responsibility for 4.3 Contract Review, and the quality function would take responsibility for 4.17 Internal Quality Audits and 4.14 Corrective and Preventive Action. Although the personnel in these functions may do a good job of ensuring that these elements operate within their scope of responsibility, they often don't see how these requirements are linked to or affect other departments or functions.

Many organizations arranged into this functional view, also known as "silos," operate by passing problems on to the next function or department. Often, those in the next function think about the problem, delay, and eventually take action. They may be able to fix what has been sent to them, or they may return the problem to the first department for more information, thus delaying the schedule of activities.

The trouble with the functional view of management is that it fails to assess the business from an entire "systems" perspective necessary for determining the information and activity interfaces between departments. For example, what information does customer service need from sales in order to initiate an order? What information does engineering need to provide to production in order to produce a product? Who needs to be involved in the review of customer requirements? Finally, where does the customer fit into all of this?

In 1997, ISO surveyed a random sample of companies to determine what changes needed to be made to the next revision of the ISO 9000 series. Users complained that the 1994 version was cumbersome, functionally oriented, manufacturing-biased, and nonsystematic, and it failed to link methods for a unified business approach. Users also felt that the year 2000 revision for ISO 9001 should have a process-oriented structure, be customer-focused, and be designed to promote continual improvement.

With this feedback in mind, the ISO Technical Committee 176 Subcommittee 2 developed a process model to depict generic requirements of a quality management system as linked processes *(refer to DIS ISO 9001:2000)*. The model shows that customer input is significant in defining requirements and that it's necessary to evaluate and verify that the requirements are met.

The process model concept is also based on eight quality management principles *(refer to Chapter 5, Transition Planning, for a definition of the principles)*:

- Customer-focused organization
- Leadership
- Involvement of people
- Process approach
- System approach to management
- Continual improvement
- Factual approach to decision making
- Mutually beneficial supplier relationships

ISO 9001:2000 attempts to address the basics of a unified approach by breaking down organizational activities into four blocks, which emphasize the process approach in the following order:

- *Management responsibility*—Management must define the requirements.
- *Resource management*—Management must determine and apply the necessary resources.
- *Product realization*—Management must ensure that processes are established and implemented.
- *Measurement, analysis and improvement*—Management must implement measurements, analyze them, and use the information from the system as a basis for improvement.

Figure 1 shows the four blocks with the corresponding elements from ISO 9001:1994.

Structuring the organization into these four blocks enables an organization to shift from functional management to process management.

Figure 2, the systems model, describes an additional view of process management.

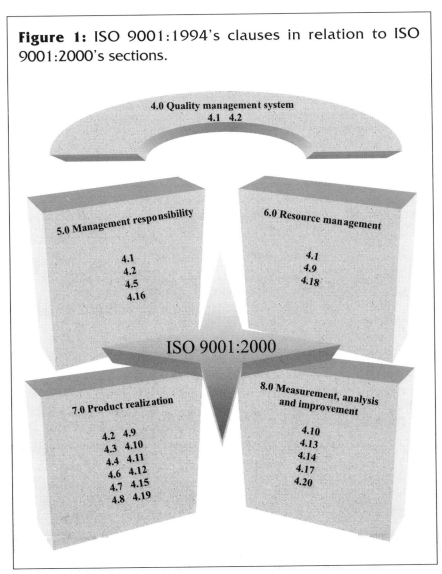

Figure 1: ISO 9001:1994's clauses in relation to ISO 9001:2000's sections.

Figure 2: The systems model of process management.

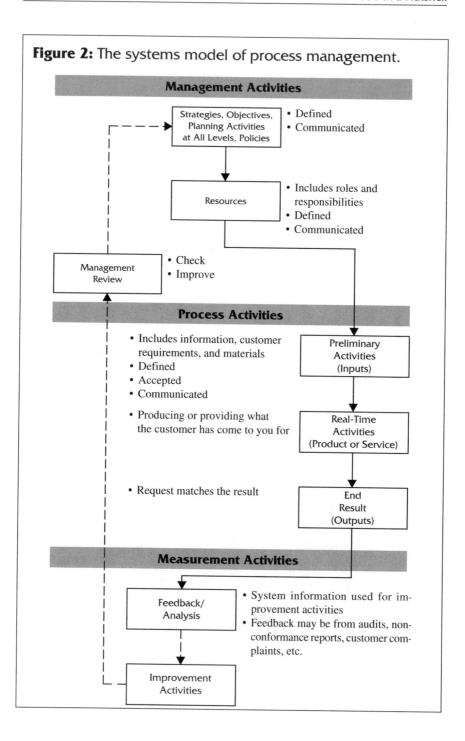

Take the following quiz to determine whether your organization operates from a functional perspective or a process perspective:

1. My organization analyzes existing methods and links between departments and personnel.
a. Always
b. Sometimes
c. Seldom
d. Never

2. Management communicates specific plans for how the quality objectives can be achieved at all levels.
a. Always
b. Sometimes
c. Seldom
d. Never

3. Departments within my organization are willing to work on cross-functional approaches to improve.
a. Always
b. Sometimes
c. Seldom
d. Never

4. Measurement results are communicated, analyzed, and used for improvement activities.
a. Always
b. Sometimes
c. Seldom
d. Never

5. Decisions for improvement activities occur before problems are discovered.
a. Always
b. Sometimes
c. Seldom
d. Never

6. Information is easily exchanged between departments.
a. Always
b. Sometimes
c. Seldom
d. Never

7. My organization clearly understands how each activity within a process affects others, as well as the effect each process has on the entire business.
a. Always
b. Sometimes
c. Seldom
d. Never

8. The personnel in my organization have clearly defined requirements from our customers and understand how to meet their needs and expectations.
a. Always
b. Sometimes
c. Seldom
d. Never

9. Top management takes an active role in reviewing the quality management system, initiating actions for improvements and ensuring that these actions are carried through.
a. Always
b. Sometimes
c. Seldom
d. Never

10. My organization has a formal system for collecting customer satisfaction and dissatisfaction data and uses this information for improvement.
a. Always
b. Sometimes
c. Seldom
d. Never

To score your quiz, count the number of times you selected each letter. Award yourself 5 points for each *a*, 3 points for each *b*, 1 point for each *c*, and 0 points for each *d*. Add your points together for a total.

If you scored 40–50 points, your organization is doing a good-to-excellent job of thinking and managing in process terms. If you scored 35–39 points, your organization may be working toward a process approach but is not doing so consistently. If you scored fewer than 35 points, you are still in a functional mode of management.

PROCESS MANAGEMENT BASICS

The following section covers some of the basic concepts of process management. Let's start with two process definitions:

1. A process is a course, direction, trend, sequence, or method.
2. A process is an end-to-end set of activities that is customer-focused and cross-functional, and it delivers a product and/or service that creates value for the customer.

Both definitions must be considered because all organizations have processes and customers. However, if processes or methods are not clearly defined, end-to-end breakdowns will occur, and ultimately customers will be dissatisfied.

Processes are inherent in all organizations. It would be impossible to produce a product or service without processes. Those organizations that have marginal processes can continue to exist; however, those with *linked* processes are most likely more competitive, innovative, and consistently profitable.

Although organizations that don't have linked processes may be able to address their customers' needs, the degree to which they are able to satisfy their end customers is demonstrated in their ability to consistently execute their processes. For example, suppose that personnel at XYZ Co. tell you that they're far too creative to be locked into disciplines or procedures. What you may discover about XYZ Co. is that its processes or methods are loosely connected, and breakdowns occur frequently between and within departments or functions. Because its methods are not defined, the organization cannot really assess how well it's able to repeat its processes. When product gets out the door, XYZ's personnel consider it a success and don't see the path of destruction or dollars lost in achieving their goal. The path of destruction often shows up in such things as customer complaints, nonconforming product, and employee burnout.

If all organizations have processes, then why change the standard and make such a big deal about process management? Even though organizations have methods in place, the ability to consistently meet their customers' expectations has plagued organizations for years. ISO 9001:2000's mission is to provide a stepping stone from functional management thinking to process management thinking. ISO 9001:2000 is structured to facilitate the idea that all processes are linked. Often, organizations look at the nonconforming product or the customer complaint and implement immediate solutions rather than challenging the process. As some organizations recognize, without a connected approach, they operate as if they're playing golf in the dark. Satisfying customers becomes a guessing game: No one knows for certain which hole is being played, what the course looks like, or which club to use. Instead of knowing precisely what comes next, these organizations feel their way along, hoping that the club they're pulling from their bag is the right one.

Organizations that are already registered are not exempt from this dilemma. Some have become registered with weak, disconnected systems. Although they may be working to improve these systems, the emphasis on continually reviewing processes and making the necessary changes may have waned since the certificate arrived.

The necessity for organizations to structure their business as a connected series of events is crucial, and the following four factors need to be considered when moving toward process management.

First, defining and documenting what your organization really does helps you gain an understanding of the methods in place. Unfortunately, documentation gets a bad rap, but until you visually observe the flow of activities, it's next to impossible to reach agreement about and establish a clear picture of the steps. This is a time for honesty and full participation; documentation is not a task that involves only the management representative. Without an analysis of the systems, the methods that were minimally defined in the first place provide little insight when solving problems. When organizations don't take the time to define the details, they can't assess how well they're doing or pinpoint the real cause of problems. The sheer effort of working around systems simply to get products or services out the door on time becomes the mode of operation.

Next, determine how the processes link together and who's responsible for them. It's amazing how many employees still don't have a clear definition of their responsibility within their jobs. The idea that organizations can turn all of their employees into mini-entrepreneurs, and that everyone is a leader, is a misguided approach. This approach can lead to disruption because no one is sure who is handling which responsibilities. Therefore, every company needs to define its leaders and doers—which leads to the third point.

Management must provide the direction. This means not only business and market direction, but also people direction. For example, it's not uncommon for three different positions to be responsible for the same task. In the event of a crisis, however, no one claims responsibility, which leads to blaming and finger pointing. Consequently, managers need to be decisive and must take responsibility for guiding the system, much like the conductor of an orchestra leads talented, creative people through the interpretation of musical scores.

Finally, managers must use the information that comes from this well-orchestrated system to determine where changes and improvements need to be made. The most important point is that management must take action. Without analysis and action, the system will remain open-ended, and problems will continue to occur even though the system has been defined.

In summary, organizations that adopt process or systems thinking can effectively adapt to changing markets and competitive conditions, share best practices across all levels, and implement continuous improvement efforts. This systems view of organizations shows the interactions and the sequence of business activities between customers and organizational functions. The personnel understand what their responsibilities are, where they fit into the process, and how their performance affects the entire system. With clearly established roles and responsibilities, organizations can link performance results with their processes.

Chapter 3

Comparing ISO 9001:1994 with ISO 9001:2000

U sers of ISO 9000 are very familiar with the numbering scheme and structure of the 1994 version. This chapter shows a comparison of ISO 9001:1994's requirements to ISO 9001:2000 by using the 1994 version's 4.1–4.20 clause structure. It's arranged in an easy-to-follow format for quick reference. Each section, by clause, includes:

■ *1994 Requirements*—a paraphrase of ISO 9001:1994's requirements

■ *What's New*—clarifications and an explanation of ISO 9001:2000's new requirements, broken down by the new numbering scheme, 4–8. The reference to the appropriate ISO 9001:2000 section is listed in parentheses.

■ *What's the Same*—a list of requirements that are the same in ISO 9001:1994 and ISO 9001:2000

■ *What's Not Included*—a list of ISO 9001:1994's requirements that are not included in ISO 9001:2000. Because ISO 9001:2000 has yet to be subjected to real-world auditing, be careful when updating your quality management system. Even when a requirement from ISO 9001:1994 is no longer explicitly stated, it's possible that auditors may still expect organizations to preserve that aspect of their quality management system.

■ *In a Nutshell*—a summary of the changes as they apply to each of ISO 9001:1994's clauses

4.1 MANAGEMENT RESPONSIBILITY

1994 Requirements

■ Top management must define and document the organization's quality policy, quality objectives, and commitment to quality.

■ The quality policy must be relevant to the organization's goals as well as the customers' needs and expectations.

■ The quality policy must be understood, implemented, and maintained at all levels of the organization.

■ The responsibility, the authority, and the interrelation of all personnel that affect quality must be defined and documented for those personnel who need the organizational freedom to initiate action to prevent nonconformities; to identify and record problems; to initiate, recommend, and provide solutions; to verify the implementation of solutions; and to control processes until the nonconformity has been corrected.

■ Top management must identify and provide resources, including trained personnel, for management, for carrying out work activities, and for verification activities, including audits.

■ Top management must appoint a management representative who has the defined authority to:

- ensure that the quality system is established, implemented, and maintained in accordance with the standard.
- report on the quality system performance during the management review and use the results as a basis for improvement.

■ Top management must review the quality system at defined intervals.

■ Top management must ensure the suitability and effectiveness of the quality system related to the standard and stated quality policy and objectives.

■ The management reviews must be recorded and the records maintained.

4.1 MANAGEMENT RESPONSIBILITY

WHAT'S NEW

5 Management responsibility

Clarifications

■ It's more explicitly stated that management must establish the quality policy and quality objectives. The management review should be used to evaluate the need for changes to the quality management system, quality policy, and quality objectives. *(Reference 5.1 Management commitment; 5.6.1 General)*

■ The quality policy must be communicated and understood at "appropriate" levels within the organization rather than at "all levels." *(Reference 5.3 Quality policy)*

■ Top management has the responsibility for and must provide evidence of their commitment to ensure the availability of resources. *(Reference 5.1 Management commitment)*

■ More than one management representative may be designated. *(Reference 5.5.3 Management representative)*

New Requirements

■ Top management must provide evidence of their commitment to system development and improvement, which includes communicating to the organization the importance of meeting customer, regulatory, and legal requirements. *(Reference 5.1 Management commitment)*

■ Top management must ensure that customer needs and expectations are determined and fulfilled. *(Reference 5.2 Customer focus)*

■ Top management must ensure that the quality policy:
  - includes a commitment to meeting requirements and continual improvement.
  - provides framework for quality objectives.
  - is reviewed for ongoing suitability.
  - is a controlled document.
    (Reference 5.3 Quality policy)

■ Quality objectives must be established at relevant functions and levels. They must be measurable and consistent with the quality policy.

4.1 MANAGEMENT RESPONSIBILITY

Objectives must include those needed to meet product requirements. *(Reference 5.4.1 Quality objectives).*

■ Top management must define functions and their interrelations and assign responsibilities and authorities to appropriate personnel to facilitate effective quality management. *(Reference 5.5.2 Responsibility and authority)*

■ The management representative has the authority and responsibility to promote the awareness of customer requirements throughout the organization. *(Reference 5.5.3 Management representative)*

■ Organizations must ensure that communication takes place between various levels and functions regarding the effectiveness of the quality management system and the related processes. *(Reference 5.5.4 Internal communication)*

■ Management reviews must cover specific inputs and outputs during the review. The management review must also evaluate any changes that could affect the quality management system, including the quality policy and quality objectives. *(Reference 5.6 Management review)*

■ Inputs to the management review must include:
  • audit results
  • feedback from customers
  • analyses of process performance and product conformance
  • preventive and corrective actions status
  • follow-up actions from previous management reviews
  • any changes that might affect the quality management system
  (Reference 5.6.2 Review input)

■ Outputs of the management review must include actions relating to:
  • the quality management system (and its processes) improvement
  • product improvement (related to customer requirements)
  • resource needs
  (Reference 5.6.3 Review output)

4.1 MANAGEMENT RESPONSIBILITY

6 Resource management

Clarifications

■ Organizations must ensure that personnel with defined responsibilities in the quality management system are competent; that is, they possess appropriate levels of education, training, skills, and experience. *(Reference 6.2.1 Assignment of personnel)*

New Requirements

■ Organizations must determine and provide, in a timely manner, the resources necessary to implement and improve the quality management system processes and to address customer satisfaction. *(Reference 6.1 Provision of resources)*

7 Product realization

Clarifications

■ Organizations must provide resources and facilities that are specific to the product. *(Reference 7.1 Planning of realization processes)*

New Requirements

■ None

8 Measurement, analysis and improvement

Clarifications

■ None

New Requirements

■ The standard is more specific in its requirements for attaining improvement. Organizations must facilitate continual improvements through the use of the quality policy, objectives, and management review. *(Reference 8.5.1 Planning for continual improvement)*

4.1 MANAGEMENT RESPONSIBILITY

WHAT'S THE SAME

■ Organizations must establish and document a quality policy and quality objectives and their commitment to them.

■ The quality policy must be relevant to organizational goals and customer requirements.

■ The quality policy must be disseminated throughout the organization.

■ Responsibilities and authorities must be defined and communicated.

■ Top management must allocate adequate resources to the quality management system.

■ The management representative must be a member of top management who has defined responsibility and authority on matters relating to the quality system.

■ Top management is responsible for the periodic quality system review to ensure its suitability and effectiveness.

■ Management review records must be kept.

WHAT'S NOT INCLUDED

■ The specific list of actions for personnel who affect quality is no longer listed in ISO 9001:2000.

■ Responsibility and authority for personnel "that affect quality" has been removed.

■ The specific language regarding types of resources (i.e., trained personnel) for management, for performance of work, and for verification activities, including audits, has been removed.

IN A NUTSHELL

Top management is responsible for all aspects of defining, documenting, and communicating the organization's quality policy. The quality policy must demonstrate management's "commitment" to meeting requirements and continual improvement. ISO 9001:2000 ensures that there is alignment between the quality policy, the quality objectives, and the organizational and customer requirements.

4.1 MANAGEMENT RESPONSIBILITY

The specific activities of personnel have been eliminated from the responsibility and authority clause (ISO 9001:1994 4.1.2.1). Therefore, organizations will need to be clear in determining what responsibilities and authorities are necessary for "effective" quality management. ISO 9001:2000 has reduced the scope of this requirement, thus allowing organizations to become more flexible in defining who does what within the quality management system.

Top management has the ultimate responsibility for ensuring that adequate resources are provided throughout the organization to effectively implement and improve the organization's quality management system. The organization must ensure that personnel are competent based on their education, training, skills, and experience. Furthermore, the organization must determine and provide resources to implement and improve the quality management system and to address customer satisfaction.

The management representative now has the additional responsibility of promoting the awareness of customer requirements throughout the organization. It is up to the organization to determine how the management representative will "promote" this awareness. There is also now the possibility that more than one person can represent the organization for the purposes of the quality management system.

The purpose of the management review process is to periodically evaluate the performance and effectiveness of the quality management system. The main intent of these reviews is to determine the health of the quality management system by identifying opportunities for improvement and determining actions to facilitate the improvement. ISO 9001:2000 specifies inputs and outputs to the management review process, including evaluating changes that could affect the quality system. Furthermore, it directly links the management review process to the continual improvement of the organization.

4.2 QUALITY SYSTEM

1994 REQUIREMENTS

■ A documented quality system must be developed by creating and documenting quality procedures and work instructions and effectively implementing them.

■ The quality manual must make reference to all the documented quality system procedures relating to the ISO 9001 requirements and include an outline of the structure of the documentation used.

■ Organizations must effectively implement the quality system and its procedures.

■ Organizations must define and document how they meet their quality requirements.

■ Quality planning must be in accordance with the organizations' specifications for their products, projects, or contracts.

WHAT'S NEW

4 Quality management system
Clarifications

■ ISO 9001:2000 requires the establishment, documentation, implementation, maintenance, and continual improvement of the organization's quality management system. *(Reference 4.1 General requirements)*

■ The range and extent of the quality management system procedures depend on:
  • the organization's size and type
  • the complexity and interaction of the organization's processes
  • the competence of the organization's personnel
  (Reference 4.2 General documentation requirements)

■ Organizations must establish and implement documentation (other than that required by ISO 9001:2000) for the effective operation and control of their processes. *(Reference 4.2 General documentation requirements)*

4.2 QUALITY SYSTEM

New Requirements
■ ISO 9001:2000 is more specific about what organizations must consider when implementing their quality management system. In order to implement a quality management system, organizations must:
- identify processes
- determine process sequence and interaction
- establish the criteria and methods necessary to ensure effective operation and control of processes
- ensure information availability necessary to support processes
- measure, monitor, and analyze processes

(Reference 4.1 General requirements)

5 Management responsibility
Clarifications
■ Quality manuals must include the scope of the quality management system, including exclusions, the documented procedures (or a reference to them), and the description for the sequence and interaction of processes. *(Reference 5.5.5 Quality manual)*
■ Quality manuals must be controlled. *(Reference 5.5.5 Quality manual)*

New Requirements
■ Quality planning includes the following items:
- quality management system processes
- necessary resources
- quality management system continual improvement

(Reference 5.4.2 Quality planning)

■ Organizational planning must ensure that organizational change is conducted in a controlled manner and that the quality management system's integrity is maintained during this change. *(Reference 5.4.2 Quality planning)*

4.2 QUALITY SYSTEM

6 Resource management
Clarifications
■ None

New Requirements
■ None

7 Product realization
Clarifications
■ When planning realization processes, organizations must:
  • set quality objectives
  • establish processes and documentation
  • provide resources and facilities
  • maintain records necessary to provide confidence of conformance
  (Reference 7.1 Planning of realization processes)

New Requirements
■ None

8 Measurement, analysis and improvement
Clarifications
■ None

New Requirements
■ None

WHAT'S THE SAME
■ Organizations must implement a quality management system.
■ Organizations must document their quality management system with procedures defined in a quality manual.
■ Organizations must prepare documented procedures consistent with the standard.

4.2 QUALITY SYSTEM

WHAT'S NOT INCLUDED

■ An outline of the documentation structure is no longer specified.

■ As listed in 4.2.3 Quality Planning, the activities related to quality planning that were to be considered are no longer listed.

IN A NUTSHELL

The general intent for this section is the same as the 1994 version's clause 4.2; however, ISO 9001:2000 introduces the word "process." This introduction implies the use of a process-management approach for the organization. Throughout ISO 9001:2000, it's stated that processes are created to manage the ISO 9001 requirements. The new process-based structure of the standard is consistent with the Plan-Do-Check-Act improvement cycle. Under 4.2 General documentation requirements, Note 1 states that a procedure must be established, documented, implemented, and maintained only where the words "documented procedure" appear in ISO 9001:2000 *(see Chapter 5, Transition Planning)*.

In the 1994 version, confusion existed around quality planning and quality plans. The revised standard has given more specific guidelines for planning and has more clearly described "quality plans" in a note under 7.1 Planning of realization processes.

Organizations are required to have documented quality planning activities. The outputs from these activities form the foundation for the organizational processes needed to meet the established quality objectives. ISO 9001:2000 doesn't give a list of items to consider as appropriate. Instead, under 5.4.2 Quality planning, the standard lists three areas that organizational planning must cover. A new requirement specifies that quality planning must ensure that organizational change happens in a controlled and sustainable manner. Through documented quality planning, organizations create a path to attain the desired results.

4.3 CONTRACT REVIEW

1994 REQUIREMENTS

- Organizations must document procedures for contract review.
- Customer requirements must be defined and documented.
- Organizations must review contracts prior to acceptance to ensure that there are clear requirements, that any differences are resolved, and that the order requirements can be met.
- Orders received orally must have requirements agreed upon before acceptance.
- Organizations must determine how contract amendments are handled and how this amended information is disseminated to the correct personnel.
- Contract review records must be maintained.

WHAT'S NEW

5 Management responsibility
Clarifications
- None

New Requirements
- Top management must ensure that customer needs/expectations are defined and the requirements are transferred and met to achieve customer satisfaction. *(Reference 5.2 Customer focus)*

6 Resource management
Clarifications
- None

New Requirements
- None

7 Product realization
Clarifications
- The results of the review and follow-up actions must be recorded. *(Reference 7.2.2 Review of product requirements)*

4.3 CONTRACT REVIEW

■ Relevant documentation must be amended when changes occur. *(Reference 7.2.2 Review of product requirements)*

New Requirements
■ Defining the customer requirements has been expanded to include requirements for availability, delivery, and support as well as regulatory and legal requirements. *(Reference 7.2.1 Identification of customer requirements)*
■ Organizations must identify and implement arrangements for customer communication relating to product information, order handling, and customer feedback, including complaints. *(Reference 7.2.3 Customer communication)*

8 Measurement, analysis and improvement
Clarifications
■ None

New Requirements
■ None

WHAT'S THE SAME
■ Organizations must review contracts prior to order acceptance to ensure the requirements are clearly defined, that requirements can be met, and that any differences are resolved prior to acceptance.
■ Contract amendment information must be disseminated to the correct personnel.
■ Contract review records must be maintained.

WHAT'S NOT INCLUDED
■ Documented procedures for contract review are no longer specifically stated.

4.3 CONTRACT REVIEW

IN A NUTSHELL

The ISO 9001:2000 contract review requirements are basically the same as in ISO 9001:1994. Some of the wording has changed; however, the general intent is the same. The new standard has expanded the idea of contract review. Organizations must determine customer requirements, identify and implement arrangements for customer communication, and convert these requirements into products and/or services that will achieve customer satisfaction. More information on this topic can be found in Chapter 4, Noteworthy Changes.

4.4 DESIGN CONTROL

1994 REQUIREMENTS

■ Organizations must maintain procedures that control and verify product designs to ensure that they meet specified requirements.

■ Organizations must develop plans for design activity that designate the personnel responsible for implementation. The responsible personnel must be qualified and have adequate resources.

■ The design plans must be updated as the design evolves.

■ Defined organizational and technical interfaces must exist that document, transmit, and regularly review necessary information.

■ The design-input activities must be identified, documented, and reviewed for adequacy.

■ Responsible personnel must resolve any conflicts or ambiguities in the input requirements.

■ Organizations must consider the results of contract review activities as design input.

■ Design-output must be documented in terms that are verified and validated against design-input requirements.

■ The design output must meet design-input requirements, contain or reference acceptance criteria, identify critical product characteristics, and be reviewed prior to release.

■ Pertinent personnel must plan and conduct formal documented reviews and maintain records of the reviews.

■ Organizations must conduct design verification to ensure design-stage output meets the design-stage input requirements.

■ Design verification measures must be recorded.

■ Organizations must conduct design validation to ensure that the product conforms to defined user needs/requirements.

■ Changes and modifications throughout the design process must be identified, documented, reviewed, and approved before implementation.

WHAT'S NEW

5 Management responsibility
Clarifications
■ None

4.4 DESIGN CONTROL

New Requirements
■ None

6 Resource management
Clarifications
■ None

New Requirements
■ None

7 Product realization
Clarifications
■ The interfaces between different groups must be "managed" to ensure effective communication and clarity of responsibilities. *(Reference 7.3.1 Design and/or development planning)*
■ Planning requirements are more specific and require that the design and/or development planning determine the review, verification, and validation appropriate at each stage. *(Reference 7.3.1 Design and/or development planning)*
■ The results of the review and follow-up actions must be recorded. *(Reference 7.3.4 Design and/or development review)*
■ The results of verification and follow-up actions must be recorded. *(Reference 7.3.5 Design and/ or development verification)*
■ The results of the review of changes and follow-up actions must be documented. *(Reference 7.3.7 Control of design and/or development changes)*

New Requirements
■ Design and/or development input requirements must include functional and performance requirements, requirements derived from previous similar designs, and any other requirements essential for design and development. *(Reference 7.3.2 Design and/or development inputs)*
■ Design and/or development outputs must provide relevant information for production and service operations. *(Reference 7.3.3 Design and/or development outputs)*

4.4 DESIGN CONTROL

■ The design and/or development reviews must be conducted to evaluate the capability to fulfill requirements, to identify any problems, and to propose follow-up actions. *(Reference 7.3.4 Design and/or development review)*

■ Where applicable, the validation must be completed prior to delivery or implementation of the product and/or service. If full validation is impossible prior to delivery, partial validation must be taken to the maximum extent practical. Validation results and follow-up actions must be recorded. *(Reference 7.3.6 Design and/or development validation)*

■ Organizations must determine the effect of the changes on the constituent parts and delivered products. As appropriate, the changes must be verified and validated before implementation. *(Reference 7.3.7 Control of design and/or development changes)*

8 Measurement, analysis and improvement
Clarifications
■ None

New Requirements
■ None

WHAT'S THE SAME
■ Organizations must plan and control the design and/or development of a product or service.
■ Design input information must be reviewed for adequacy, and conflicting requirements must be resolved.
■ Design output must be documented in terms that can be verified and validated against design-input requirements.
■ The design output must meet design-input requirements, contain or reference acceptance criteria, identify critical product characteristics, and be reviewed prior to release.
■ Pertinent personnel must plan and conduct formal documented reviews and maintain records of the reviews.

4.4 DESIGN CONTROL

■ Organizations must conduct design and/or development verification to ensure that design-stage output meets the design-stage input requirements.

■ Organizations must conduct design and/or development validation to ensure the product conforms to intended customer use.

■ Changes and modifications throughout the design and/or development process must be documented and approved before implementation.

WHAT'S NOT INCLUDED

■ The 1994 requirement to define interfaces between different groups is no longer specified.

IN A NUTSHELL

The main purpose of each of the subclauses of the 1994 version of 4.4 Design Control has been addressed in ISO 9001:2000. Additional requirements have been added to further ensure that organizations clearly understand what their customer requirements are before they begin the design process. For example, the design input and output requirements are more specifically stated. Organizations will be required to consider the effect of design changes on several items. Furthermore, the results of these changes and any associated actions must be documented.

4.5 DOCUMENT AND DATA CONTROL

1994 REQUIREMENTS

■ Organizations must maintain procedures for controlling quality system documentation and data, which include external documents.

■ Documents and data must be reviewed and approved for adequacy. A master list or similar tool must be established to ensure revision control and to prevent the inadvertent use of obsolete documents.

■ Pertinent issues of documents must be available.

■ Invalid or obsolete documents must be promptly removed.

■ Obsolete documents that are retained must be identified.

■ Document and data changes must be reviewed and approved by the same personnel that performed the original review and approval.

■ Where practical, the nature of the change must be identified.

WHAT'S NEW

5 Management responsibility
Clarifications
■ The control of external documents must include the identification and distribution of these documents. *(Reference 5.5.6 Control of documents)*

New Requirements
■ The procedure for the control of documents must include a provision for ensuring that documents remain legible, readily identifiable, and retrievable. *(Reference 5.5.6 Control of documents)*
■ Documents defined as records must be controlled. *(Reference 5.5.6 Control of documents)*

6 Resource management
Clarifications
■ None

New Requirements
■ None

4.5 DOCUMENT AND DATA CONTROL

7 Product realization
Clarifications
■ None

New Requirements
■ None

8 Measurement, analysis and improvement
Clarifications
■ None

New Requirements
■ None

WHAT'S THE SAME
■ Organizations must maintain documented procedures for controlling quality system documentation, including external documents. These external documents must be identified and recorded.
■ Organizations must be able to identify current revision status of documents.
■ Documents must be approved for adequacy prior to release. Revision control must be used to prevent the inadvertent use of obsolete documents.
■ Obsolete documents must be identified, if retained.
■ Documents must be reviewed, updated as necessary, and re-approved.
■ The note in the 1994 version including all types of media is now found in Note 2 in 4.2 General documentation requirements.

WHAT'S NOT INCLUDED
■ The requirement that document and data changes must be reviewed and approved by the same personnel that performed the original review and approval is no longer specified.

4.5 DOCUMENT AND DATA CONTROL

■ It's no longer specified that the nature of the changes must be identified within the document or appropriate attachments.
■ The specific reference to a master list has been removed.

IN A NUTSHELL

There are no significant changes regarding document control. The main intent of the 1994 version's 4.5 Document and Data Control is included, except that the word "data" has been omitted. However, the control of data is implied in the final statement, which specifies that documents defined as records must be controlled. In ISO 9001:2000, an organization must identify the current revision of a document, although it does not specify how it needs to be done (e.g., master list).

4.6 PURCHASING

1994 REQUIREMENTS

■ Organizations must maintain procedures to ensure that purchased product conforms to specified requirements.

■ Subcontractors must be selected and evaluated based on their ability to meet quality system requirements.

■ The extent and control over subcontractors must be based on product type, quality impact on the final product, and demonstrated capability.

■ Records of acceptable subcontractors must be maintained.

■ Purchasing documents must clearly describe the product that is ordered and must be reviewed and approved prior to release.

■ Organizations may verify purchased product at a subcontractor location after verification arrangements and the product release method have been specified.

■ Customers may verify purchased product at the organization's subcontractor location if contractually specified. In this case, organizations are still responsible for providing acceptable products to their customers.

WHAT'S NEW

5 Management responsibility
Clarifications
■ None

New Requirements
■ None

6 Resource management
Clarifications
■ None

New Requirements
■ None

4.6 PURCHASING

7 Product realization
Clarifications
■ In order to eliminate confusion caused in the 1994 edition, the term "supplier" has replaced the term "subcontractor" and the term "organization" has replaced the term "supplier." *(Reference 3 Terms and definitions)*
■ The "review and approval" requirement of purchasing documents prior to release has been replaced by a requirement for "ensuring the adequacy" of purchasing documents prior to release. *(Reference 7.4.2 Purchasing information)*
■ There is now one joint requirement for the organization or customer verification of purchased product at a supplier's location. Verification arrangements and the method of product and/or service release are still required in purchasing documents. *(Reference 7.4.3 Verification of purchased product)*
■ Organizations must establish the criteria upon which suppliers will be chosen and define their periodic evaluation. The results of these evaluations and any related actions must be documented. *(Reference 7.4.1 Purchasing control)*

New Requirements
■ None

8 Measurement, analysis and improvement
Clarifications
■ None

New Requirements
■ None

WHAT'S THE SAME
■ Organizations must maintain purchasing processes to ensure that purchased product conforms to specified requirements.
■ Subcontractors must be selected and evaluated based on their ability to supply product and/or service in accordance with organizational

4.6 PURCHASING

requirements. Records of subcontractor activity must be maintained.
■ The extent and control over subcontractors must be based on the quality impact on the final product.
■ Purchasing documents must clearly describe the product that is ordered and must be reviewed prior to release.
■ Organizations or their customers may verify purchased product at a subcontractor location after verification arrangements and the product release method have been specified.

WHAT'S NOT INCLUDED
■ The paragraph that describes, where applicable, purchasing data, including type, class, grade, or other product identification; title or positive identification; applicable specifications; drawings; process requirements; inspection instructions; and other relevant technical data has been removed.
■ Basing the control of subcontractors on the type of product, the subcontractor's previously demonstrated capability, and audit records and reports is no longer specified.
■ The customer's verification of a subcontractor does not pardon the organization from the responsibility to provide acceptable product, is no longer a requirement.

IN A NUTSHELL
The purpose of ISO 9001:1994's 4.6 Purchasing has remained the same; however, the section focused on control over suppliers has been modified. The terminology has been improved to eliminate confusion surrounding the terms "subcontractor" and "supplier." Several of the items that were required "where applicable" on purchasing documents have been eliminated. Organizations will still need to consider what criteria they use for supplier selection and how often their suppliers should be evaluated. Overall, the purchasing section still focuses on ensuring that purchased product conforms to specifications and that purchasing documents clearly describe what is being ordered.

4.7 CONTROL OF CUSTOMER-SUPPLIED PRODUCT

1994 REQUIREMENTS

■ Organizations must have procedures for how they control products supplied by their customers for incorporation into the organizations' products.

■ Organizations are responsible for the proper maintenance, control of verification, and storage of their customers' products.

■ Organizations must record and report lost, damaged, or unsuitable customer-supplied products to their customers.

■ Although organizations must verify customer-supplied products, the customer is still responsible for providing acceptable products.

WHAT'S NEW

5 Management responsibility
Clarifications
■ None

New Requirements
■ None

6 Resource management
Clarifications
■ None

New Requirements
■ None

7 Product realization
Clarifications
■ The terminology now used is to "exercise care" with customer property while it is under the organization's supervision and/or in use by the organization. *(Reference 7.5.3 Customer property)*
■ Organizations must "identify, verify, protect, and maintain" customer property. *(Reference 7.5.3 Customer property)*

4.7 CONTROL OF CUSTOMER-SUPPLIED PRODUCT

■ The note in this section states that customer property may also include property of an intellectual nature, which is defined as information provided to organizations by customers in confidence. *(Reference 7.5.3 Customer property)*

New Requirements
■ None

8 Measurement, analysis and improvement
Clarifications
■ None

New Requirements
■ None

WHAT'S THE SAME
■ Organizations are responsible for the proper maintenance and storage of customer-supplied product, and any damage must be documented and reported to their customers.

WHAT'S NOT INCLUDED
■ A documented procedure for customer-supplied products is no longer specified.

IN A NUTSHELL
There are no significant changes in this section. The words "identify and protect" have been added to the requirements for clarification. Organizations are still completely responsible when handling customer property. Any problems with the customer's property are documented and the customer is notified. The term "property" is now used in place of "product."

4.8 PRODUCT IDENTIFICATION AND TRACEABILITY

1994 REQUIREMENTS

■ Where applicable, organizations must maintain documented procedures for the suitable identification of product from receipt through production, delivery, and installation.

■ If required in a customer contract, organizations must maintain documented procedures for the unique identification of individual product and batches. The unique identification must be recorded.

WHAT'S NEW

5 Management responsibility
Clarifications
■ None

New Requirements
■ None

6 Resource management
Clarifications
■ None

New Requirements
■ None

7 Product realization
Clarifications
■ The 4.12 Inspection and Test Status requirement has been included in this section. The intent remains the same, although the description of the requirement has been reduced significantly. *(Reference 7.5.2 Identification and traceability)*

■ Organizations must not only record the unique identification but also control it. *(Reference 7.5.2 Identification and traceability)*

4.8 PRODUCT IDENTIFICATION AND TRACEABILITY

New Requirements
■ None

8 Measurement, analysis and improvement
Clarifications
■ None

New Requirements
■ None

WHAT'S THE SAME
■ Where applicable, organizations must suitably identify products throughout production and service operations.
■ The unique identification number must be recorded where traceability is a requirement.

WHAT'S NOT INCLUDED
■ The requirement to establish documented procedures for identifying products is no longer specified.
■ The specified requirement for documented procedures in relation to unique identification of individual product and batches has been removed.

IN A NUTSHELL
In ISO 9001:2000, the 1994 version's 4.8 Product Identification and Traceability and 4.12 Inspection and Test Status are combined under one section. The intent is that organizations will use these requirements, as applicable, for their processes.

4.9 PROCESS CONTROL

1994 Requirements

■ Organizations must identify and plan the production, installation, and servicing processes that directly affect quality and ensure that these processes are carried out under controlled conditions.

■ Organizations must provide documented work instructions and specify workmanship criteria.

■ Organizations must use, maintain, and approve suitable equipment and provide a suitable working environment.

■ Organizations must monitor and control process parameters and product characteristics.

■ Organizations must remain in compliance with reference standards/codes, quality plans, and documented procedures.

■ For special processes, organizations must use qualified personnel and maintain records for qualified processes, equipment, and personnel.

What's New

5 Management responsibility
Clarifications
■ None

New Requirements
■ None

6 Resource management
Clarifications
■ None

New Requirements
■ Organizations must identify, provide, and maintain facilities necessary to achieve conformity of their products. *(Reference 6.3 Facilities)*

■ Organizations must identify and manage human and physical factors in relation to the work environment. *(Reference 6.4 Work environment)*

4.9 PROCESS CONTROL

7 Product realization
Clarifications
- Organizations must plan the sequence of processes that will result in product realization. The quality plan consists of the documentation that describes these processes within the quality management system. (*Reference 7.1 Planning of realization processes*)

New Requirements
- Organizations must have available the information that defines the characteristics of the products and/or services that are to be achieved. (*Reference 7.5.1 Operations control*)
- "Special processes" must be validated to demonstrate the ability of the processes to achieve planned results. (*Reference 7.5.5 Validation of processes*)
- Organizations must address the arrangements for validation, as applicable for special processes. (*Reference 7.5.5 Validation of processes*)

8 Measurement, analysis and improvement
Clarifications
- None

New Requirements
- None

WHAT'S THE SAME
- Organizations must plan and control their production and service operations.
- Work instructions and specifications must be clear and documented.
- Processes must be monitored.
- Organizations must use and maintain suitable equipment.
- For special processes, organizations must use qualified personnel and maintain records for qualified processes, equipment, and personnel.

4.9 PROCESS CONTROL

What's Not Included

■ Controlled conditions that are no longer referenced include:
- criteria for workmanship
- approval of processes and equipment, as appropriate
- compliance with reference standards/codes, quality plans, and documented procedures.

In a Nutshell

Section 7.5 Production and service operations incorporates some of the requirements of the ISO 9001:1994 clauses, such as 4.19 Servicing, as well as most of the requirements of 4.9 Process Control. Organizations are still required to maintain operations in a controlled environment and provide work instructions for personnel (where necessary). There are several new requirements, however, that expand on some of the basic requirements in the 1994 version. Organizations must now consider how they validate and revalidate special processes where the resulting output cannot be verified by subsequent measuring. They also must consider the facilities (6.3) and work environment (6.4) *(see Chapter 4, Noteworthy Changes).*

4.10 INSPECTION AND TESTING

1994 REQUIREMENTS

■ Organizations must maintain procedures for inspection and testing activities to ensure that products conform to specified requirements.

■ Organizations must inspect or verify incoming product conformance to specifications prior to being used.

■ Organizations must determine the amount of required receiving inspection based on the control of suppliers as well as documented evidence of specification conformance.

■ Organizations must positively identify any product released for urgent production in the event of recall.

■ Organizations must inspect and test all in-process products per the documented procedures, and no product is to be released until all inspection and test activities have been performed successfully.

■ Organizations must ensure that all final inspection and testing is conducted in accordance with documented procedures. These procedures require that all incoming and in-process tests were completed.

■ Product is to be released only after all activities specified in the documented procedures are completed and the data and documentation is available and authorized.

■ Organizations must maintain records to show that their products have been inspected. The records must show that the products either passed or failed. Records must identify who is responsible for releasing products.

WHAT'S NEW

5 Management responsibility
Clarifications
■ None

New Requirements
■ None

4.10 INSPECTION AND TESTING

6 Resource management
Clarifications
■ None

New Requirements
■ None

7 Product realization
Clarifications
■ The terminology "inspection and testing" has now been changed to "monitoring or verification activities." Organizations are responsible for implementing monitoring activities *(Reference 7.5.1 Operations control)*, determining verification and validation activities, and establishing the criteria for acceptability *(Reference 7.1 Planning of realization processes)*.
■ Organizations must define and implement processes for release, delivery, and post-delivery activities. This is a combination of 4.10 Inspection and Testing; 4.15 Handling, Storage, Packaging, Preservation, and Delivery; and 4.19 Servicing from ISO 9001:1994. *(Reference 7.5.1 Operations control)*

New Requirements
■ None

8 Measurement, analysis and improvement
Clarifications
■ Organizations must define, plan, and implement measurement and monitoring activities to assure conformity at appropriate stages of the product realization processes. *(Reference 8.1 Planning)*
■ Organizations must apply methods for monitoring processes necessary to meet customer requirements. The methods must ensure the ongoing ability of the process to meet the intended purpose. *(Reference 8.2.3 Measurement and monitoring of processes)*

4.10 INSPECTION AND TESTING

■ Organizations must measure and monitor product characteristics to ensure that requirements are met. *(Reference 8.2.4 Measurement and monitoring of product)*

New Requirements
■ None

WHAT'S THE SAME

■ The specific breakdown of inspection activities, i.e., receiving, in-process, final, and record requirements, is no longer explicit in the standard, although ISO 9001:2000 *implies* that inspection activities must be carried out.
■ Product release cannot proceed until all activities are satisfactorily carried out.
■ Organizations must document evidence of conformity with the acceptance criteria.
■ Organizations must maintain records of the authority responsible for the release of the product.

WHAT'S NOT INCLUDED

■ The specific reference to receiving, in-process, final, and inspection requirements is no longer included.
■ The requirement that records must show both pass and fail status is no longer stated—only conformity is specified.

IN A NUTSHELL

Quite a bit of ISO 9001:1994's 4.10 Inspection and Testing's text has been moved to ISO 9004:2000; however, the purpose of 4.10 has remained. Organizations are required to determine what measurement and monitoring methods will be employed to ensure that both process and product and/or service requirements are met. ISO 9001:2000 doesn't explicitly specify inspection and testing activities for incoming, in-process, and final product. There still must be documented evidence

4.10 INSPECTION AND TESTING

that products and/or services conform to specifications, and evidence must show what acceptance criteria is used. When addressing monitoring and verification requirements, it will be important to review all of the applicable sections of the revised standard to meet the requirements.

4.11 CONTROL OF INSPECTION, MEASURING, AND TEST EQUIPMENT

1994 REQUIREMENTS

■ Organizations must establish and maintain documented procedures.

■ Equipment must be used in a way that ensures that measurement uncertainty is known and is consistent with required measurement capability.

■ If organizations use test software or comparative references for inspection, they must be checked for proof of capability for verification activities and rechecked at selected intervals. The extent and frequency of such checks must be determined by the organization, and records must be maintained.

■ Organizations must make technical data pertaining to measurement equipment available to their customers if necessary to determine if equipment is functioning adequately.

■ Organizations must:

- Determine measurements and accuracy required for equipment.
- Ensure that equipment is capable of measuring to the needed accuracy and precision.
- Identify all inspection, measuring, and test equipment that will affect the quality of the product.
- Ensure that their equipment is calibrated at specified intervals, or prior to use, against certified equipment traceable to international or national standards.
- Define the process for calibration, including details of equipment type, unique identification, location, frequency of checks, check method, acceptance criteria, and action to be taken when results are unsatisfactory.
- Identify equipment to show calibration status.
- Maintain records.
- Assess previous inspections for validity when equipment used is out of calibration.
- Ensure that environmental conditions are suitable for the calibrations and inspections.
- Ensure that equipment is handled, preserved, and stored to maintain accuracy and fitness for use.
- Safeguard inspection, measuring, and test facilities from adjustments that would invalidate the calibration.

4.11 CONTROL OF INSPECTION, MEASURING, AND TEST EQUIPMENT

WHAT'S NEW

5 Management responsibility
Clarifications
■ None

New Requirements
■ None

6 Resource management
Clarifications
■ None

New Requirements
■ None

7 Product realization
Clarifications
■ The results of calibration must be recorded. ISO 9001:1994 only stated that the calibration records for inspection, measuring, and test equipment must be maintained.
■ The control of production and service operations must include the availability and use of measuring and monitoring devices. *(Reference 7.5.1 Operations control)*

New Requirements
■ None

8 Measurement, analysis and improvement
Clarifications
■ None

New Requirements
■ None

4.11 CONTROL OF INSPECTION, MEASURING, AND TEST EQUIPMENT

WHAT'S THE SAME

■ Organizations must identify measurement needs and devices to use and must also ensure that the measurement capability is consistent with the measurement requirements.

■ Measurement devices must be calibrated against known traceable standards, or, where no standard exists, the basis for calibration must be recorded.

■ Adjustments must not invalidate calibration.

■ Measurement devices must be protected from damage and deterioration.

■ Organizations must maintain calibration records.

■ Out-of-calibration results must be reassessed for validity, and corrective action must be taken.

■ The note referencing ISO 10012 remains the same.

WHAT'S NOT INCLUDED

■ The methods for establishing and maintaining documented procedures is no longer specified.

■ The requirement that test software and hardware be rechecked at prescribed intervals and that the extent and frequency of the checks be defined is no longer specified.

■ The requirement that records be kept for the test software/hardware checks is no longer stated.

■ Specifics are no longer provided for defining the process employed for the calibration of inspection, measuring, and test equipment, including details of equipment type, unique identification, location, frequency of checks, check method, or acceptance criteria.

■ The requirement for equipment to be identified with a suitable indicator or record to show calibration status is no longer included.

■ Requirements for suitable environmental conditions for carrying out calibrations, measurements, etc. have been removed.

4.11 CONTROL OF INSPECTION, MEASURING, AND TEST EQUIPMENT

IN A NUTSHELL

One significant change in the revised standard is the term "where applicable" for the specific ISO 9001:1994 a–e requirements as applied to organizations' measuring and monitoring devices. ISO 9001:2000 does not make it clear whether organizations can determine which of the requirements apply to their devices and ignore the others. This may be one of those gray areas that will require interpretation by registrars.

Another difference in ISO 9001:2000 is the elimination of a reference to test hardware. The revised standard no longer specifies some of the specific requirements that some companies found helpful when setting up their systems, such as detailing equipment type, unique identification, location, and frequency and method of checks. The elimination of these details could cause more confusion than clarification.

Finally, two key requirements are no longer included in the standard: identifying equipment with a suitable indicator to show the calibration status and ensuring that the environmental conditions for carrying out the calibrations, inspections, and measurement are suitable.

Although the fundamental purpose of ISO 9001:1994's clause 4.11 has remained the same, ISO 9001:2000 has lightened the requirements. Organizations will need to consider whether anything will change with their existing calibration systems. It's strongly suggested that these systems remain intact to preserve the same discipline and routine that was required by ISO 9001:1994.

4.12 INSPECTION AND TEST STATUS

1994 REQUIREMENTS

■ The inspection and test status of products must be identified.

■ The identification must indicate conformance or nonconformance of the product in regard to inspections and tests performed.

■ The identification must be defined in the quality plan or procedures.

■ The identification must be maintained throughout production, installation, and servicing to ensure that only conforming product is released, used, or installed.

WHAT'S NEW

5 Management responsibility

Clarifications
■ None

New Requirements
■ None

6 Resource management

Clarifications
■ None

New Requirements
■ None

7 Product realization

Clarifications
■ None

New Requirements
■ None

4.12 INSPECTION AND TEST STATUS

8 Measurement, analysis and improvement
Clarifications
■ None

New Requirements
■ None

WHAT'S THE SAME
■ Organizations must identify the status of product as related to measurement and monitoring requirements.

WHAT'S NOT INCLUDED
■ The requirement that inspection status indicate conformance and nonconformance is no longer stated.
■ Identification of inspection and test status no longer needs to be defined in the quality plan or in a documented procedure.
■ The requirement that only product that has passed inspection is released is no longer specified.

IN A NUTSHELL
The inspection and test status requirements from ISO 9001:1994 are not explicitly stated in ISO 9001:2000, though the purpose of inspection status appears in 7.5.2 Identification and traceability and in 7.5.1 Operations control (defined processes for release). It's simply a good business practice to know the inspection status of product throughout production, service, or installation to ensure that only conforming product is used, released, or installed. Organizations that practice this are advised to continue. Organizations that are considering adopting ISO 9001:2000 should carefully review their systems to ensure that they have sound practices in place for the status of the product as relates to inspection and testing. In particular, these practices should clearly address conforming and nonconforming product to prevent the shipment of nonconforming product.

4.13 CONTROL OF NONCONFORMING PRODUCT

1994 REQUIREMENTS

■ Organizations must document procedures to ensure that nonconforming product is prevented from being used unintentionally. The procedures must describe methods for identification, documentation, evaluation, segregation (when possible), disposition, and communication to the appropriate parties.

■ The responsibility for review and authority for the disposition must be defined.

■ Nonconforming product must be reviewed according to documented procedures.

■ If contractually required, use or repair of nonconforming products must be reported to customers, and records must be kept describing the nonconformity and repairs.

■ Repaired and reworked product must be re-inspected according to procedures or quality plans.

WHAT'S NEW

5 Management responsibility
Clarifications
■ None

New Requirements
■ The review of product conformance is now a requirement for management review. *(Reference 5.6.2 Review input)*

6 Resource management
Clarifications
■ None

New Requirements
■ None

4.13 CONTROL OF NONCONFORMING PRODUCT

7 Product realization
Clarifications
- None

New Requirements
- None

8 Measurement, analysis and improvement
Clarifications
- Nonconforming product that is corrected is subject to reverification; however, ISO 9001:2000 does not specify that it must be done in accordance with the quality plan and/or documented procedures. *(Reference 8.3 Control of nonconformity)*

New Requirements
- If organizations discover nonconforming products after delivery or after use has started, they must take action. *(Reference 8.3 Control of nonconformity)*

WHAT'S THE SAME
- Nonconforming products must be identified and controlled to prevent unintended use.
- Organizations must have documented procedures for controlling nonconforming products.
- Organizations must re-inspect repaired or reworked products.

WHAT'S NOT INCLUDED
- The definition of responsibility for review and authority for the disposition of nonconforming product is no longer specified.
- It is no longer specified that nonconforming products must be reviewed in accordance with procedures that define types of dispositions used.
- The records describing the nonconformance accepted by the customer are no longer specified.

4.13 CONTROL OF NONCONFORMING PRODUCT

■ The details for control of nonconforming product (e.g., documentation, evaluation, disposition, and notification of functions concerned) are no longer included.

IN A NUTSHELL

Overall, the message of ISO 9001:1994's 4.13 Control of Nonconforming Product has remained the same: Product that does not conform to specified requirements should not be used or shipped. The requirements for the control of nonconforming product no longer contain the specific requirements for review and disposition of nonconforming product, as in ISO 9001:1994. However, the intent here also remains the same. A new requirement has been added for organizations to address nonconforming product that is detected after delivery. Specifically, organizations must take action related to the consequences of nonconformity.

ISO 9001:2000 has removed the "where required by contract" in front of the section relating to the reporting of the repair of nonconforming product to the customer. Instead, the passage now states that organizations are "often required" to report the "rectification" (correction or revision) to the customer, end-user, regulatory body, or other body.

4.14 CORRECTIVE AND PREVENTIVE ACTION

1994 REQUIREMENTS

■ Procedures for implementing corrective and preventive actions must be documented.

■ Any actions taken to eliminate cause must be appropriate for the size of the problem.

■ Any changes to documented procedures resulting from corrective or preventive actions must be recorded.

■ Procedures for corrective action must include handling effectively customer complaints and product nonconformities; investigating the cause of nonconformities (includes product, process, system); recording the results of the investigation; determining actions to be taken to eliminate actual problem; and devising methods for ensuring that the actions taken are effective.

■ Procedures for preventive action must include the use of relevant information to detect, analyze, and eliminate potential causes of problems; the steps required to implement preventive action; methods of ensuring that actions taken are effective; and evidence that information on actions taken is submitted to management review.

WHAT'S NEW

5 Management responsibility
Clarifications
■ ISO 9001:2000 now explicitly requires that the status of corrective and preventive actions be reviewed during management review. *(Reference 5.6.2 Review input)*

New Requirements
■ None

6 Resource management
Clarifications
■ None

4.14 CORRECTIVE AND PREVENTIVE ACTION

New Requirements
■ None

7 Product realization
Clarifications
■ None

New Requirements
■ Organizations must define communication requirements for customer complaints. *(Reference 7.2.3 Customer communication)*

8 Measurement, analysis and improvement
Clarifications
■ The procedure for corrective action must define requirements for corrective action activities. *(Reference 8.5.2 Corrective action)*
■ Organizations must define methods for obtaining and using information for customer complaints (dissatisfaction). ISO 9001:1994 only required the effective handling of customer complaints. *(Reference 8.2.1 Customer satisfaction)*
■ Corrective action must prevent recurrence of problems and preventive actions must prevent occurrence of problems. *(Reference 8.5.2 Corrective action; 8.5.3 Preventive action.)*
■ The results of the corrective action taken, instead of the results of the investigation, must be recorded. *(Reference 8.5.2 Corrective action)*

New Requirements
■ Organizations must continually improve their management systems and use corrective and preventive action as a basis for facilitating improvements. *(Reference: 8.5.1 Planning for continual improvement)*
■ Organizations must now record the results of the preventive actions. *(Reference 8.5.3 Preventive action)*

4.14 CORRECTIVE AND PREVENTIVE ACTION

WHAT'S THE SAME

■ The purpose of ISO 9001:1994's requirements has, for the most part, remained the same.

■ The requirement for documented procedures has remained.

WHAT'S NOT INCLUDED

■ The requirement to implement and record changes to the documented procedures resulting from corrective or preventive action is no longer stated.

■ The requirement for submitting preventive actions to management review has been moved to the Management Review section. *(Reference 5.6.2 Review input)*

■ The reference to "application of controls" to ensure that corrective or preventive actions are effective has been eliminated and replaced with a requirement to review and record the results of the actions taken.

■ The requirement to record the results of the investigation of corrective action has been changed; the standard now requires recording the results of the corrective action itself.

■ The references to specific sources of information (i.e., audit results, quality records, etc.) to detect, analyze, and eliminate potential causes have been removed.

IN A NUTSHELL

The discussion of corrective and preventive action in ISO 9001:1994 has been reworded rather than changed. Corrective and preventive actions are now specifically referred to as one of the tools that organizations must use to facilitate improvements. Furthermore, by requiring that the review of these actions be part of management reviews, ISO 9001:2000 clearly establishes top management's responsibility for the improvement of the organization. It also states that actions taken must prevent recurrence. When reviewing actions taken over time, organizations must ensure that repeat occurrences are addressed.

4.14 CORRECTIVE AND PREVENTIVE ACTION

Due to the greater emphasis on documenting the results of corrective and preventive actions, organizations should consider what format will be the easiest to use and understand. Many organizations document the problem-solving steps involved for the investigation of nonconformities using some type of methodology. Typically, this methodology includes problem identification, root-cause analysis, determination and implementation of corrective and preventive actions, follow-up, and closure. This information is documented and considered a quality record, which should be submitted in a summary format for management review.

4.15 HANDLING, STORAGE, PACKAGING, PRESERVATION, AND DELIVERY

1994 REQUIREMENTS

■ Organizations must have documented procedures for handling, storage, packaging, preservation, and delivery.

■ Organizations must provide methods for handling product to prevent damage and deterioration.

■ Organizations must use designated storage areas or stock rooms to prevent damage/deterioration of product prior to delivery.

■ Methods must be in place for receiving and removing product from storage areas.

■ The condition of product in storage must be assessed at regular intervals.

■ Organizations must control their packing, packaging, and marking processes, including the materials used to ensure that their customers' needs are met.

■ Appropriate methods of preserving and segregating the product must be applied.

■ Organizations must arrange for the protection of the product after final inspection and testing. If contractually agreed upon, the protection must extend to delivery of product to the final destination.

WHAT'S NEW

5 Management responsibility
Clarifications
■ None

New Requirements
■ None

6 Resource management
Clarifications
■ None

New Requirements
■ None

4.15 HANDLING, STORAGE, PACKAGING, PRESERVATION, AND DELIVERY

7 Product realization
Clarifications
■ Organizations must ensure that their customers' requirements continue to be met from internal processing through final delivery. This must include identification, handling, storage, packaging, and protection of product. *(Reference 7.5.4 Preservation of product)*
■ ISO 9001:1994 stated that when contractually specified, protection of product must be extended to include delivery to destination. ISO 9001:2000 now requires the implementation of defined processes for delivery. *(Reference 7.5.1 Operations control)*

New Requirements
■ The requirement extends to parts or components of a product or service. *(Reference 7.5.4 Preservation of product)*

8 Measurement, analysis and improvement
Clarifications
■ None

New Requirements
■ None

WHAT'S THE SAME
■ A system must be in place to ensure that the product or service is not affected during internal processing and final delivery.

WHAT'S NOT INCLUDED
■ The requirement for documented procedures is not explicit for handling, storage, packaging, preservation, and delivery.
■ The methods for handling product to prevent damage and deterioration are not specifically stated.
■ The requirement to use designated storage areas or stock rooms to prevent damage/deterioration of product prior to delivery is no longer specified.

4.15 HANDLING, STORAGE, PACKAGING, PRESERVATION, AND DELIVERY

■ The methods for receiving and removing product from storage areas are not specifically stated.

■ The requirement that the condition of products in storage be assessed at regular intervals is no longer stated.

■ The requirement for organizations to control packing, packaging, and marking processes, including the materials used to ensure that their customers' needs are met, has been removed.

■ The requirement for organizations to apply appropriate methods of preserving and segregating products is no longer specified.

■ The requirement for organizations to protect product to final delivery has been removed.

IN A NUTSHELL

The requirements for handling, storage, packaging, preservation, and delivery have been considerably broadened. Most of the requirements from ISO 9001:1994 for this section have been placed in ISO 9004:2000. The user is advised to read the corresponding section in ISO 9004:2000 when developing a quality management system, especially the section concerning handling, storage, packaging, preservation, and delivery. Because the specific requirements have been reduced, it's unclear what auditors will be looking for with regard to system documentation.

4.16 CONTROL OF QUALITY RECORDS

1994 REQUIREMENTS

■ Organizations must have documented procedures for the identification, collection, indexing, access, filing, storage, maintenance, and disposition of records.

■ Records must be maintained to demonstrate conformance to requirements and the effective operation of the quality system.

■ Pertinent subcontractor records must be included.

■ Records must be legible and stored and retained so they are readily retrievable.

■ A suitable environment must be provided to prevent damage, deterioration, and loss.

■ Record retention times must be established and recorded.

■ When contractually agreed upon, records must be available for evaluation by the customer or representative for an agreed period.

WHAT'S NEW

5 Management responsibility
Clarifications
■ ISO 9001:2000 explicitly requires that records be controlled. *(Reference 5.5.7 Control of quality records)*

New Requirements
■ None

6 Resource management
Clarifications
■ None

New Requirements
■ The requirement for organizations to keep training records has been broadened to include records of education, experience, training, and qualifications. *(Reference 6.2.2 Training, awareness and competency)*

4.16 CONTROL OF QUALITY RECORDS

7 Product realization

Clarifications
- None

New Requirements
- The following records were included in ISO 9001:1994; however, the requirement to record results and follow-up actions has been added:
  - Records must be kept to provide confidence that processes and resulting products conform. *(Reference 7.1 Planning of realization processes)*
  - Records for contract review must be more explicit. Rather than having a general record requirement, ISO 9001:2000 specifies that the results of the review and follow-up actions must be recorded. *(Reference 7.2.2 Review of product requirements)*
  - Reviews at all suitable stages of design and/or development must be conducted. The results of the design and/or development reviews and subsequent follow-up actions must be recorded. *(Reference 7.3.4 Design and/or development review)*
  - The results of verification and subsequent follow-up actions must be recorded. *(Reference 7.3.5 Design and/or development verification)*
  - The results of validation and subsequent follow-up actions must be recorded. *(Reference 7.3.6 Design and/or development validation)*
  - The results of the review of changes and subsequent follow-up actions must be recorded. *(Reference 7.3.7 Control of design and/or development changes)*
  - The results of supplier evaluations and follow-up actions must be recorded. *(Reference 7.4.1 Purchasing control)*
  - The results of calibration must be recorded. *(Reference 7.6 Control of measuring and monitoring devices)*

4.16 CONTROL OF QUALITY RECORDS

8 Measurement, analysis and improvement
Clarifications
■ Records must be kept for preventive action. *(Reference 8.5.3 Preventive action)*

New Requirements
■ None

WHAT'S THE SAME
■ Organizations must have a documented procedure that explains their record-keeping system.
■ The following records are still required in ISO 9001:2000:
- Management reviews *(Reference 5.6.3 Review output)*
- Training *(Reference 6.2.2 Training, awareness and competency)*
- Contract review *(Reference 7.2.2 Review of product requirements)*
- Subcontractor evaluations *(Reference 7.4.1 Purchasing control)*
- The unique identification of products where traceability is a requirement *(Reference 7.5.2 Identification and traceability)*
- Customer property that is lost, damaged, or unsuitable for use *(Reference 7.5.3 Customer property)*
- Qualified processes *(Reference 7.5.5 Validation of processes)*
- Calibration records for inspection, measuring, and test equipment. *(Reference 7.6 Control of measuring and monitoring devices)*
- Where no standards exist, the basis used for calibration *(Reference 7.6 Control of measuring and monitoring devices)*
- Results of internal audits *(Reference 8.2.2 Internal audit)*
- Follow-up activities that verify corrective action implementation *(Reference 8.2.2 Internal audit)*
- Results of corrective actions *(Reference 8.5.2 Corrective action)*

WHAT'S NOT INCLUDED
■ The requirement for collection, indexing, access, and filing has been removed.
■ The requirement for records of nonconformities accepted by the customer is no longer stated.

4.16 CONTROL OF QUALITY RECORDS

■ The specific reference to subcontractor records in 4.16 has been removed.

■ The legibility requirement of records has been removed but is implied in 5.5.6 Control of documents.

■ The requirement for a suitable environment to prevent damage, deterioration, and prevention of loss has been removed.

■ The requirement for making records available to the customer under contract is no longer stated.

■ The note that reminds the user that records can be any type of media has been removed, but it's implied in a note in 4.2 General documentation requirements.

IN A NUTSHELL

Many of the previous record requirements have stayed in place. However, subtle wording changes imply that more than just the evidence of a record will be required. For instance, under both customer information and design, results of the review and follow-up actions will need to be recorded. In the past, most organizations could show that the record existed. ISO 9001:2000 requires auditors to look more closely at the results and actions of the activities instead of just at the paperwork.

4.17 INTERNAL QUALITY AUDITS

1994 REQUIREMENTS

■ Organizations must have documented procedures for planning and implementing internal quality audits.

■ Internal audits must be scheduled.

■ Internal audits must be carried out by independent personnel.

■ Internal audit results must be recorded.

■ Those responsible for the areas being audited must be informed of the audit results.

■ Management must take timely corrective action on problems found during the audit.

■ Follow-up activities must verify and record that the corrective actions taken are implemented and effective.

WHAT'S NEW

5 Management responsibility

Clarifications

■ The standard more explicitly states that internal audit results must be a part of the management reviews. Management reviews must include actions relating to the internal audit results. This requirement appeared in the note under internal audits in ISO 9001:1994. *(Reference 5.6.2 Review input)*

New Requirements

■ None

6 Resource management

Clarifications

■ None

New Requirements

■ None

4.17 INTERNAL QUALITY AUDITS

IN A NUTSHELL

All of the requirements have been carried over from ISO 9001:1994. The revision requires organizations to review their internal audit procedures to ensure the inclusion of responsibilities, requirements, and methodologies for conducting the audits. Audit results are now an explicit requirement for management review and for the facilitation of continual improvement activities.

The auditing techniques that internal auditors use may change slightly. Namely, auditors will need to determine a methodology of system auditing that takes a cross-functional, process-oriented approach to developing checklists, conducting audits, and reporting the results. It's recommended that internal auditors receive additional training, as appropriate, on new auditing techniques for ISO 9001:2000.

4.18 TRAININ

1994 REQUIREM

■ Organizations must have documented
training needs and providing training to
affecting quality.
■ Personnel performing assigned work
■ Records of the training must be maint

WHAT'S NEW

5 Management responsibility
Clarifications
■ None

New Requirements
■ None

6 Resource management
Clarifications
■ Those who are assigned responsibilit
management system must be competent b
ing, skills, and experience. *(Reference 6.*
■ Training must meet the competency
performing activities affecting quality
awareness and competency)

New Requirements
■ The requirement for organizations to
expanded to include records of educati
qualifications. *(Reference 6.2.2 Training*
■ Employees must understand the relev
they do and how they contribute to th
objectives. *(Reference 6.2.2 Training, a*
■ Organizations must evaluate the effe
provide. *(Reference 6.2.2 Training, awa*

7 Pro
Clarif
■ No

New R
■ No

8 Mea
Clarif
■ No

New R
■ No

■ Org
• D
• P
• M
• Q

■ A d

In a
person
the effe
A gray
qualifi
synony
may no
organiz

4.17 INTERNAL QUALITY AUDITS

7 Product realization
Clarifications
■ None

New Requirements
■ None

8 Measurement, analysis and improvement
Clarifications
■ ISO 9001:2000 clarifies the following:
  • The purpose of the internal audits is to determine whether the management system conforms to the standard and if the system has been effectively implemented and maintained.
  • The schedule must also be based on previous audit results.
  • The audit must be conducted by those who do not perform the activity being audited instead of those with direct responsibility.
  • The audit procedure must include the responsibilities and requirements for conducting audits, the audit scope, audit frequency, and the methodologies used, which must be recorded.
  (Reference 8.2.2 Internal audit)

New Requirements
■ Audit results must be used to facilitate continual improvement. *(Reference 8.5.1 Planning for continual improvement)*

WHAT'S THE SAME
■ All requirements from ISO 9001:1994 have been carried over to the revision.

WHAT'S NOT INCLUDED
■ None

4.17 INTERNAL QUALITY AUDITS

IN A NUTSHELL

All of the requirements have been carried over from ISO 9001:1994. The revision requires organizations to review their internal audit procedures to ensure the inclusion of responsibilities, requirements, and methodologies for conducting the audits. Audit results are now an explicit requirement for management review and for the facilitation of continual improvement activities.

The auditing techniques that internal auditors use may change slightly. Namely, auditors will need to determine a methodology of system auditing that takes a cross-functional, process-oriented approach to developing checklists, conducting audits, and reporting the results. It's recommended that internal auditors receive additional training, as appropriate, on new auditing techniques for ISO 9001:2000.

4.18 TRAINING

1994 REQUIREMENTS

■ Organizations must have documented procedures for identifying training needs and providing training to those who perform activities affecting quality.

■ Personnel performing assigned work must be qualified.

■ Records of the training must be maintained.

WHAT'S NEW

5 Management responsibility

Clarifications

■ None

New Requirements

■ None

6 Resource management

Clarifications

■ Those who are assigned responsibilities defined within the quality management system must be competent based on their education, training, skills, and experience. *(Reference 6.2.1 Assignment of personnel)*

■ Training must meet the competency levels required of personnel performing activities affecting quality. *(Reference 6.2.2 Training, awareness and competency)*

New Requirements

■ The requirement for organizations to keep training records has been expanded to include records of education, experience, training, and qualifications. *(Reference 6.2.2 Training, awareness and competency)*

■ Employees must understand the relevance and importance of what they do and how they contribute to the achievement of the quality objectives. *(Reference 6.2.2 Training, awareness and competency)*

■ Organizations must evaluate the effectiveness of the training they provide. *(Reference 6.2.2 Training, awareness and competency)*

4.18 TRAINING

7 Product realization
Clarifications
- None

New Requirements
- None

8 Measurement, analysis and improvement
Clarifications
- None

New Requirements
- None

WHAT'S THE SAME
- Organizations must:
  - Determine training needs
  - Provide training to meet these needs
  - Maintain records of training
  - Qualify their personnel

WHAT'S NOT INCLUDED
- A documented procedure for training is no longer specified.

IN A NUTSHELL
In addition to addressing training needs and qualifications of personnel, organizations must now describe how they will determine the effectiveness of their training and the competency of their people. A gray area of this section is the difference between competence and qualification. Although "competence" and "qualification" are synonyms, many would agree that individuals can be qualified but may not necessarily be competent to carry out the job. Consequently, organizations should consider defining what competency means to them

4.18 TRAINING

and how they would demonstrate this within their quality management system. Organizations must also ensure that their employees are aware of the importance of their activities and how they, as individuals, contribute to achieving the quality objectives. Also, ISO 9001:2000 now specifies what types of training records must be kept *(see Chapter 5, Transition Planning)*.

4.19 SERVICING

1994 REQUIREMENTS
■ Organizations must have documented procedures for performing, verifying, and reporting that servicing meets specified conditions when servicing is a requirement.

WHAT'S NEW

5 Management responsibility
Clarifications
■ None

New Requirements
■ None

6 Resource management
Clarifications
■ None

New Requirements
■ None

7 Product realization
Clarifications
■ Organizations must have defined processes for applicable post-delivery activities. *(Reference 7.5.1 Operations control)*

New Requirements
■ None

8 Measurement, analysis and improvement
Clarifications
■ None

New Requirements
■ None

4.19 SERVICING

WHAT'S THE SAME

■ See "In a Nutshell."

WHAT'S NOT INCLUDED

■ See "In a Nutshell."

IN A NUTSHELL

ISO 9001:1994's requirements for servicing as it relates to repairs, maintenance, or other services specified in the original contract, and which is to take place after delivery, are blended into section 7.5.1, Operations control. ISO 9001:2000 no longer specifically addresses the need for documented procedures when performing, verifying, and reporting the servicing aspect, as was interpreted from ISO 9001:1994.

4.20 STATISTICAL TECHNIQUES

1994 REQUIREMENTS

■ Organizations must identify the statistical techniques necessary to establish, control, and verify process capability and product characteristics.

■ Organizations must have documented procedures for the implementation and use of the statistical techniques identified.

WHAT'S NEW

4 Quality management system
Clarifications
■ None

New Requirements
■ Organizations must measure, monitor, and analyze the processes they establish and implement actions to ensure continual improvement. *(Reference 4.1 General requirements)*

5 Management responsibility
Clarifications
■ None

New Requirements
■ None

6 Resource management
Clarifications
■ None

New Requirements
■ None

7 Product realization
Clarifications
■ None

4.20 STATISTICAL TECHNIQUES

New Requirements
■ None

8 Measurement, analysis and improvement
Clarifications
■ Organizations must define, plan, and implement methods for measuring and monitoring activities. These activities must ensure that requirements are met and improvements achieved. ISO 9001:2000 makes it clear that measurements must be used and are not an option. *(Reference 8.1 Planning)*

New Requirements
■ Customer satisfaction must be one of the measures of an organization's quality management system performance. *(Reference 8.2.1 Customer satisfaction)*
■ The methods for obtaining and using customer satisfaction/dissatisfaction information must be defined. *(Reference 8.2.1 Customer satisfaction)*
■ Organizations must apply methods for measuring and monitoring processes to attain customer satisfaction. The methods must ensure the ability of each process to satisfy its intended purpose. *(Reference 8.2.3 Measurement and monitoring of processes)*
■ Product characteristics must be measured and monitored. *(Reference 8.2.4 Measurement and monitoring of product)*
■ Organizations must collect and analyze data to determine suitability/effectiveness of the system so improvements can be made. Measuring and monitoring activities are sources of data. *(Reference 8.4 Analysis of data)*
■ Organizations must facilitate improvement activities through the analysis of data. *(Reference 8.5.1 Planning for continual improvement)*

WHAT'S THE SAME
■ Organizations must determine the need for and application of methods, including statistical techniques.

4.20 STATISTICAL TECHNIQUES

WHAT'S NOT INCLUDED
■ A documented procedure to implement and control the application of statistical techniques is no longer specified.

IN A NUTSHELL

ISO 9001:2000 specifically requires the use of analysis and measurements to facilitate improvement activities. The 1994 version suggested that an organization first identify the need for statistical techniques, and if such a need wasn't found, the requirements didn't apply. It's apparent that measurements will need to be implemented and used to achieve conformity and for improvement activities. ISO 9001:2000 makes it clear that customer satisfaction and/or dissatisfaction is one of the measurements of performance.

For many organizations, implementation of this section will be a challenge. The maturity of an organization's measurement systems will determine the amount of effort and development needed. In other words, if organizations have measurements in place, they will need to evaluate those measurements and the results they will provide. The main point to remember is that ISO 9001:2000 focuses on using measurements and their results to drive continual improvement.

Chapter 4

Noteworthy Changes

A lthough ISO 9001:2000's new requirements were specifically identified in Chapter 3, Comparing ISO 9001:1994 with ISO 9001:2000, this chapter further explains some of the new requirements to provide additional understanding. Organizations will need to thoroughly comprehend the impact of these requirements and determine what actions are necessary to comply with ISO 9001:2000. Keep in mind that some organizations may not currently have a system in place to address these requirements.

PROCESS MODEL STRUCTURE

The most radical change in ISO 9001:2000 is the elimination of the 4.1–4.20 clause format. By using tools such as the cross-reference matrix found in this book and understanding the process approach, organizations already familiar with ISO 9001:1994 will be able to begin to make the necessary changes. Though the original purpose of the 1994 version may not have changed, ISO 9001:2000 requires careful reading as many of the terms and requirements have been modified or reworded.

MANAGEMENT AND CONTINUAL IMPROVEMENT

One of the key changes in ISO 9001:2000 requires management to use the information from the quality management system to implement improvements. The initial requirements begin under section 5.3 Quality policy, in which the standard requires management to show a commitment to quality by meeting the requirements and maintaining continual improvement. This is further emphasized in section 8.4 Analysis of data, which requires organizations to collect and analyze data to determine the effectiveness of their quality systems and to identify improvements. Finally, in section 8.5 Improvement, organizations are required to plan and manage their processes for continual improvement and must facilitate improvement activities through the use of the following:

■ Quality policy
■ Objectives
■ Audit results
■ Analysis of data
■ Corrective and preventive action
■ Management review

Although some organizations use information effectively, many organizations don't use the information from their quality management system to initiate improvement activities. These requirements may prove to be a challenge for such organizations.

5.4.2 QUALITY PLANNING

Organizations should carefully review their quality planning activities. ISO 9001:1994 implied that planning should be done, but ISO 9001:2000 section 5.4.2 Quality planning requires that the resources needed to achieve quality and the quality objectives be aligned with planning activities. Section 7.1 Planning of realization processes links quality objectives to include the requirements needed to make a product, project, or contract. Section 5.4.2 Quality planning also requires management to pay attention to changes that may occur in the organization such as implementation of computer systems, changes in management representatives, downsizing, and so on to ensure that the integrity of the quality management system remains intact during these changes.

THE VOICE OF THE CUSTOMER

One of the fundamental differences between the ISO 9001:1994 and ISO 9001:2000 is the new requirements that are specifically focused on the organization's customers. One of the criticisms of ISO 9001:1994 was that it focused on the organization and its suppliers rather than on the customer. ISO 9001:2000 includes several sections that focus directly on the customer. Following is a brief description of each:

5.2 CUSTOMER FOCUS

Although this section is short, it has a powerful message: It is the responsibility of top management to ensure that they know their customers' needs and expectations, that organizations convert this information into requirements, and that they are able to fulfill these requirements. The purpose is to achieve customer satisfaction.

Unfortunately, organizations don't always make what their customers want. Instead, they make what they think their customers want. Section 5.2 Customer focus specifically requires organizations to have a formal mechanism to determine customer requirements. For some organizations, this may be a new concept, or at least one that has not been effectively implemented.

7.2 Customer-related processes

This section is broken up into three subsections. Two of the three sections are new. Each section deals with a different aspect of customer interaction and is listed below:

■ 7.2.1 Identification of customer requirements focuses specifically on the type of customer requirements that must be determined:

- customer-specific product requirements
- availability, delivery, and support requirements
- noncustomer-specific product requirements that are necessary for intended use
- regulatory and legal requirements

■ 7.2.2 Review of product requirements is basically the same as ISO 9001:1994's 4.3 Contract Review clause. Organizations must understand their customers' requirements and have the ability to fulfill the requirements prior to accepting the order.

■ 7.2.3 Customer communication requires organizations to identify and implement communication "arrangements" (methods) with their customers. Many organizations probably do this already, but they may not have their process formalized. The information exchanged between the organization and its customers is related to products, inquiries, contracts, order handling, changes, complaints, and feedback.

8.2.1 Customer satisfaction

The ease with which organizations are able to comply with this requirement will depend on the maturity of the organizations and their relationships with their customers. It will also depend on whether the organizations have a customer satisfaction measurement system in place and how effective it is. The requirement states that organizations will monitor information on customer satisfaction and/or dissatisfaction as one of the performance measurements of their quality management systems. Furthermore, organizations must determine the methodologies for obtaining and using this information. The intent of this requirement is to ensure that organizations have a customer complaint and general feedback system in place, and that it is effective for addressing customer concerns.

INTERNAL COMMUNICATION

5.5.4 Internal communication requires organizations to focus on how they communicate information throughout their various levels and functions. Specifically, the requirement is concerned with the communication of information that pertains to the processes of the quality management system and its effectiveness. Many organizations may have a formal communication mechanism at the top and middle management levels. However, this new requirement clearly emphasizes that information is passed between all levels. In ISO 9001:1994, only the quality policy had to be communicated to all levels. Many organizations may need to consider how they share quality management system information within their workplace.

THE ORGANIZATION
6.1 PROVISION OF RESOURCES

The focus of this section is very clear: Organizations must provide needed resources to address customer satisfaction levels and implement and improve their quality management system. It will be up to the organizations to determine whether additional resources will be necessary to meet this requirement. This requirement is tied to management review, which now specifically states that the outputs from the review must include actions relating to resource needs.

6.3 FACILITIES

This section contains one of ISO 9001:2000's biggest gray areas. It requires organizations to be responsible for identifying, providing, and maintaining the facilities they need to make good products. This section includes three areas:

- Workspace and associated facilities—this implies the inclusion of the employees' work area and the building itself
- Equipment, hardware, and software—basically from ISO 9001:1994's 4.9 Process Control

• Supporting services—this may imply the inclusion of the maintenance services to maintain the facilities

The ISO 9004:2000 guideline should be reviewed for more insight into defining the facilities requirement.

6.4 WORK ENVIRONMENT

This section indicates that organizations are responsible for identifying and managing "the human and physical factors of the work environment" needed to make good products. These factors influence motivation, satisfaction, and human performance. Human factors may include opportunities for involvement, ergonomics, safety rules, and so on. Physical factors may include heat, noise, light, air flow, or cleanliness. ISO 9004:2000 provides further description of these human and physical factors.

IN A NUTSHELL

Many of the new requirements are designed to ensure that top management is involved in quality system management. This includes clearly understanding their customers' requirements and converting these requirements into quality products that ensure customer satisfaction. Furthermore, ISO 9001:2000 specifies that a process must exist for determining these customer requirements and that top management is to ensure that all personnel understand the importance of meeting customer requirements.

Organizations are now responsible for determining and implementing a communication mechanism with their customers as it pertains to inquiries, orders, and complaints of product and/or service. ISO 9001:2000 expands upon ISO 9001:1994's 4.3 Contract Review clause by ensuring that organizations are delivering the product and/or service their customers want. Furthermore, top management must ensure that people at all levels communicate information relating to the quality management system.

Finally, managers must also be specific in their intent when aligning the quality policy, objectives, and commitment with planning and improvement activities. They must ensure that the needed resources are provided in a timely manner to implement and improve processes and to address customer complaints.

Chapter 5

Transition Planning

A smooth transition to ISO 9001:2000 will require careful consideration of documentation, training, auditing, and management. Each of these is described in this chapter, along with some transition "tips." The length of time it takes organizations to successfully become compliant to ISO 9001:2000 will depend on the maturity of their quality management system, the level of management's commitment, the number of adequately assigned resources, and the solidity of their action plan.

DOCUMENTATION

One of the first questions organizations face in the transition from ISO 9001:1994 to ISO 9001:2000 is whether they will need to change their documentation structure. The answer is a resounding "no!" Organizations aren't required to change the structure (i.e., levels or tiers) or the numbering schemes of their documentation. They will, however, need to incorporate the new requirements into their current quality management system. It's essential that organizations be able to show internal and third-party auditors how the integration of ISO 9001:2000 requirements is documented.

Organizations will be able to note "permissible exclusions" as appropriate for their situations. Organizations may only exclude requirements within section 7, Product realization, that are related to the nature of the organization's product, the customer requirements, and the applicable regulatory requirements.

As was discussed earlier in this book, ISO 9001:2000 doesn't clearly state documentation requirements. However, it states that organizations must plan their processes for product realization and must determine the need for these processes and documentation. Even though this is the case, organizations should not "undocument" any parts of their existing quality management system. In fact, they are encouraged to maintain this documentation as objective evidence of their system.

Organizations should also pay close attention to the implications of ISO 9001:2000's section 4, Quality management system, which stipulates that organizations must document their quality management system. In addition, 4.1 requires organizations to identify processes and determine the sequence and interaction of these processes. To provide evidence that these tasks have been accomplished, documentation is necessary.

Section 4.2 General documentation requirements mandates that organizations include their own documentation in their quality management system to ensure effective operation and control of processes. The extent of documentation depends on the size and type of the organization, complexity and interaction of processes, and the competence of personnel. ISO 9001:2000 gives a great deal of latitude surrounding documentation, but competence of personnel may be a key factor when determining the amount of documentation needed. For example, if employees cannot demonstrate knowledge or if inconsistent practices between employees are identified and few documented procedures exist, internal or external auditors may conclude that the processes or systems are incomplete or that training isn't effective. Organizations will need to challenge the lack of documentation as well as the overabundance of documentation.

As a reminder, documentation can be in electronic form or on paper. As many organizations move toward electronic procedures and record keeping, they will need to apply access control as well as establish effective back-up systems.

Tips

■ Do a quick review of your current quality manual to ensure that it's ISO 9001:1994-compliant. Existing noncompliances with ISO 9001:1994 may cause problems as your organization tries to determine what changes need to be made.

■ Refer to the matrix in this book to help you make the correct links and cross-references to ISO 9001:2000 (see page 107).

■ Review all of the new requirements as stated in this book and in ISO 9001:2000 and determine which documentation actions, if any, are needed to become compliant.

■ Make sure that your quality manual is compliant to ISO 9001:2000 and is controlled. Keep in mind that if your organization plans to maintain its current documentation structure, the quality manual will be essential as a springboard to the rest of the documentation.

■ Develop a cross-reference matrix that shows how your organization's current documentation aligns with ISO 9001:2000 so that any existing gaps can be determined.

■ If you plan to use your organization's existing documentation numbering scheme, be sure to incorporate any new documents into that scheme.

■ If you plan to make changes to the structure of your organization's documentation for ease of understanding the standard, a logical modification would be to redesign the quality manual documentation to meet the new ISO 9001:2000 numbering scheme and make a cross-reference to existing documentation.

■ Retrain employees, as applicable, on documentation changes, and record the training.

TRAINING

In section 6.2.2 Training, awareness and competency, two new concepts emerge. First, organizations must ensure that their employees are "aware" of how their activities contribute to the achievement of organizational goals. Second, personnel must be "competent" rather than just "trained." Some might argue that these terms are essentially the same; others would say that competence implies something beyond training: Competent people can demonstrate through their actions that they have been trained successfully. ISO will issue *ISO 10015 Guidelines for Training* to assist organizations in turning their current "trained" workforces into "competent" workforces. These guidelines will provide the methodologies for achieving this objective. Keep in mind that the competency of personnel is one of the main criteria for management to consider when determining the amount of documentation needed.

With today's rapidly changing business environment, organizations must continually determine the employee training needed to provide their customers with quality products and services that meet or exceed expectations. Because customers continue to want and expect more, organizations must periodically analyze their training and competency needs. After this analysis, organizations can compare identified needs against their current performances and document the gaps.

To close the training and competency gaps, organizations first need to define their competency needs. Once these are clear, organizations can design, plan, and provide the training. After the training has been conducted, organizations should have a mechanism in place to evaluate the outcome of the training to determine effectiveness.

TIPS

■ Consider publicizing your organization's quality objectives in a format all employees can understand. Identify training objectives that will help the organization meet quality objectives.

■ Create a flowchart to show links between organizational activities and quality objectives that will clearly convey their importance and interaction.

■ Offer employees incentives based on the achievement of quality goals.

■ Make sure that your organization has accurately defined roles and responsibilities. Then define the competencies needed for quality-related tasks that match the roles and responsibilities, assess the personnel to perform the task, and develop plans to close the competency gaps.

■ Periodically re-evaluate the competency needs of personnel, particularly when business conditions cause change within the organization, and determine if any additional training is required.

■ Ensure that an evaluation system, based on established criteria, exists to verify that the required competence levels have been achieved.

■ Ensure that employees are trained on changes to the quality management system that affect their positions or departments. Include training for documentation or system revisions, and record the training.

■ Select trainers (external, on-the-job, or companywide) carefully and verify that they understand the importance of delivering training that can demonstrate a measurable outcome.

■ Ensure that training provided is evaluated for effectiveness.

AUDITING

Although the internal auditing requirements haven't changed in ISO 9001:2000, auditors will be required to have training in several additional areas. Because the process management approach is the fundamental concept for the application of ISO 9001:2000, auditors will need to be familiar with process management concepts and terminology found in ISO 9000:2000. *ISO 19011 Guideline for Auditing (Committee Draft 1)* requires certain competencies for auditors, which include an understanding of the following:

■ Structure and function of application of basic quality management system practices and processes

■ Application of quality tools (such as measurements)
■ Significance of collected information (such as records)

Auditors are also required to have specific competencies in the eight quality management principles and techniques to enable them to examine the system to determine whether the application of requirements has been properly carried out.

Although ISO 19011 is currently at a Committee Draft 1 level and modifications to these requirements may take place prior to final release of the document, these requirements are consistent with the techniques that should be considered when auditing ISO 9001:2000. Many organizations will need to assess how they are organized and determine what changes will need to be made in order to conduct their audits.

Auditors may experience difficulties because some of the requirements are no longer contained within a single clause or element. ISO 9001:1994's requirements, in most cases, weren't broken up between clauses. Auditors will need to understand how the revised requirements are structured if they are to complete a successful audit. For example, in ISO 9001:1994's section 4.9 Process Control, the requirements were contained within one clause. Now, auditors will need to consider the requirements found in 7.1 Planning of realization processes, 7.5.1 Operations control, and 7.5.5 Validation of processes to thoroughly conduct the audit *(see Appendix 2)*.

The majority of the records required by ISO 9001:2000 must show results and follow-up actions. As such, auditors will need to do more than check to see if a record exists. They will need to pay closer attention to documented results and follow-up actions.

Some requirements fall into gray areas. One of the most challenging debates about ISO 9001:2000 centers on whether all requirements are specific enough to be auditable. Because the documentation requirements are somewhat vague, it will take a skilled auditor time and dedication to determine whether a department or organization has adequately defined its quality management system.

When planning and scheduling audits, organizations will need to take into consideration how requirements are aligned so that the requirements are audited logically. This means that organizations that used to set aside one week a year to conduct all of their required audits may need to rethink their strategy to conduct a thorough audit. Organizations may also find that they will need to initially plan audits with smaller scopes to allow their auditors to gain familiarity with ISO 9001:2000.

Tips

■ Ensure that your internal auditors are familiar with the eight quality management principles upon which ISO 9001:2000 is based. *(See the section under "Management" for an explanation of the eight quality management principles.)*

■ Review audit checklists and determine which questions and approaches need to be modified to reflect ISO 9001:2000's process approach as well as to ensure that the new requirements are covered.

■ Review the audit plan and schedule to ensure that requirements are grouped together logically.

■ Take into consideration the scope of the audit. Smaller audits may allow the auditors to adjust to the revisions of the standard.

■ Ensure that the internal auditors are competent in systems auditing and understand how the system is linked.

■ Review and become familiar with the definitions and terminologies in *ISO 9000:2000 Quality management system—Fundamentals and vocabulary.*

■ Provide training for auditors on the revisions.

MANAGEMENT

ISO 9001:2000 removes responsibility for the quality management system from quality assurance. It requires top management to ensure that:

■ Customer requirements are fully understood and met in order to assure customer satisfaction.

■ Planning activities include objectives at each relevant function and level within the organization.

■ Internal communications are established.

■ Information within the system (e.g., data, internal audit results, customer measures) is used to facilitate improvement.

ISO 9001:2000 purposely directs top management to expand their role in the quality management system. ISO 9001:2000 addresses the organization as a whole, but top management's involvement will be necessary to determine the methods and policies surrounding many of the quality management system's requirements.

Management will also need to take an active role in reviewing current performance and improvement opportunities relating to changing circumstances within organizations, process and product conformance analysis, and customer satisfaction and/or dissatisfaction. Top management has the ultimate responsibility of ensuring that adequate resources are provided throughout the organization to effectively implement and maintain the quality management system.

To help organizations understand the foundation upon which ISO 9001:2000 was developed, ISO will publish a brochure titled *Quality Management Principles*. These eight quality management principles are focused on business excellence and place an emphasis on customer satisfaction. A quality management principle is a fundamental belief that is focused on the continual performance improvement of an organization through addressing the needs of customers and stakeholders. The principles are as follows:

1. *Customer-Focused Organization*—Organizations consider customers' current and future needs, fulfill customer requirements, and strive to exceed customer expectations.

2. *Leadership*—Leaders establish the organization's purpose and direction and create an environment in which people can be involved in achieving organizational objectives.

3. *Involvement of People*—An organization's people are its essence, and their involvement and abilities benefit the organization.

4. *Process Approach*—A process approach to managing resources and activities will produce the desired results.

5. *System Approach to Management*—An organization's efficiency and effectiveness can be improved by identifying, understanding, and managing a system of interrelated processes.

6. *Continual Improvement*—An organization should have continual improvement as a permanent objective.

7. *Factual Approach to Decision Making*—Organizations should analyze data and information in order to make effective decisions.

8. *Mutually Beneficial Supplier Relationships*—Both the organization and its suppliers can create value by developing mutually beneficial, interdependent relationships.

TIPS

Top management should:

■ Understand how customer needs and expectations are identified, converted into products and/or services, and communicated within the organization

■ Ensure that a system is in place to measure customer satisfaction and dissatisfaction as well as to ensure that actions are taken on the results.

■ Ascertain how customer relationships are managed and initiate improvement actions for any identified gaps.

■ Ensure that organizational objectives are linked to customer needs and expectations.

■ Create an organizational vision and translate this vision into measurable goals and objectives.

■ Empower and involve people within the organization to achieve organizational objectives.

■ Utilize the process approach for operations as well as establish responsibility and authority for managing processes.

■ Align individual process goals and the organization's key objectives.

■ Determine the links between the organization's quality policy, quality objectives, audit results, data analysis, corrective and preventive action, and management review, and determine how these links form the foundation for continual improvement.

■ Evaluate how well the organization utilizes measurements and data analysis as a basis for improvement of the quality management system.

■ Utilize the information from data analysis to assess process and system performance in order to facilitate continual improvement.

■ Evaluate the relationships with suppliers and identify areas for improvement that will be mutually beneficial.

IN A NUTSHELL

Accreditation bodies around the world have decided that ISO 9001:1994, ISO 9002:1994, and ISO 9003:1994 will be valid for three years after the official publication of ISO 9001:2000. This decision allows time for ISO 9001:2000 to be translated into native languages. Also, due to the nature of the revisions, it's expected that organizations registered to ISO 9001, ISO 9002 or ISO 9003 will need time to make the transition to ISO 9001:2000. Although organizations that are currently registered have up to three years to make the transition, they are encouraged to make the transition as soon as possible. ISO recommends that certification/ registration bodies urge their clients to make the transition to ISO 9001:2000 before their registration to the 1994 version expires. It will be the organization's responsibility to be in close contact with its registrar about specific timing requirements that the registrar may impose.

Chapter 6

Answers to
Common Concerns

This chapter provides answers to some of the most frequently asked questions about ISO 9001:2000. The chapter is divided into seven question categories:

1. Purpose and Benefits
2. Modifications to the ISO 9000 Standards Family
3. Releasing the Revisions
4. Registration Concerns
5. Auditing Issues
6. Service and Small Organizations
7. Other Information

1. PURPOSE AND BENEFITS

What is the purpose of revising the ISO 9000 standards?

ISO has issued directives that require standards to be revised on a periodic basis so that the needs of the global business community are satisfied. User surveys have found that companies are looking for closer alignment of their quality management system with the way they actually run their businesses. ISO 9001:2000 is intended to emphasize the measurement of customer satisfaction, process management utilization, and information analysis to drive continuous improvement.

What is the focus of ISO 9001:2000, and why does this benefit my organization?

Some of the most significant points of the revised standard include its emphasis on using a process-related structure, using information from the system to facilitate improvement, and including customer satisfaction in improvement activities.

Many of the criticisms of the previous versions of the ISO 9000 series focused on disconnected processes and the lack of emphasis on improvement activities. ISO 9001:2000 stresses the importance of tying information from customer satisfaction measures, audit results, corrective/ preventive action results, and other measures to management activities in order to facilitate improvement.

ISO 9001:2000 has also attempted to address the needs and interests of organizations and specific sectors (such as telecommunication, automotive, etc.) and was designed to be compatible with other management systems, such as ISO 14000.

How are financial issues addressed in ISO 9001:2000?

Financial issues are not addressed in ISO 9001:2000. However, ISO 9004:2000 does address the control of financial resources, including activities for comparing usage against plans and taking action.

I've heard that showing evidence of improvement is now a requirement. What will I be required to do to achieve this?

One of ISO 9001:2000's focuses is to ensure that information collected from the quality management system is used for the purpose of implementing improvement. Organizations can best meet this requirement by ensuring that information such as audit results, customer satisfaction/ dissatisfaction reports, and corrective/preventive action results are reviewed by management and that appropriate actions are taken. In the past, many organizations collected this information but didn't take action, such as comparing trends or looking at all information collectively, to determine where improvements could be made.

2. MODIFICATIONS TO THE ISO 9000 STANDARDS FAMILY

I've heard that there will no longer be an ISO 9002 or an ISO 9003 standard. Why?

The requirements of both of these standards will be included in ISO 9001:2000. You will be able to tailor the standard according to your organization's activities. For example, if your organization is currently registered to ISO 9002:1994, your revised ISO 9001:2000 quality system manual would be changed from the statement that 4.4 Design Control doesn't apply and be replaced with the statement that 7.3 Design and/or development does not apply to your organization.

There are other documents within the ISO 9000 family. What will happen to them?

With more than 20 standards and documents in the ISO 9000 family, there appears to be a proliferation of standards. This has been a concern of ISO 9000 users. Therefore, the revised ISO 9000 family will only consist of four core standards: ISO 9000 (formerly *ISO 8402 vocabulary)*, ISO 9001, ISO 9004, and ISO 19011 *(Auditing Guidelines)*. The ISO 9000 family also includes *ISO 10012 Measurement Control System*, which is not considered a core document. Subsequently, the other documents will become obsolete or be replaced by technical reports.

What about the guideline documents ISO 9000-3 and ISO 9004-2?

There are no plans to revise these guideline documents. The following list shows what will happen to the remainder of the ISO 9000 documents.

■ Standards that will become technical reports:
  - *ISO 10006 Project Management*
  - *ISO 10007 Configuration Management*
  - *ISO 10013 Quality Manuals*
  - *ISO 10014 Economics of Quality*
  - *ISO 10015 Education and Training*
  - *ISO 10017 Statistical Techniques*

■ ISO will also produce three brochures:
  - *Quality Management Principles*
  - *Selection and Use of the ISO 9000 Family*
  - *Handbook for Small Businesses*

■ Documents that will become responsibilities of technical committees are as follows:
  - *ISO 9000-3 Software*—Proposed to be moved to Joint Technical Committee 1/Subcommittee 7
  - *ISO 9000-4 Dependability*—Already transferred to Technical Committee 56 on Dependability

I've heard that ISO 9001:2000 and ISO 9004:2000 are a "consistent pair." What does this mean?

The term "consistent pair" refers to the ISO 9001:2000 and ISO 9004:2000 quality management standards. These two standards have been specifically designed to be compatible with one another in the upcoming revisions. Although each standard may be used independently, the overall benefits to organizations may be more extensive if the two standards are fully implemented together. For ease of use, ISO 9004:2000 includes the requirements from ISO 9001:2000, which is a significant change from the 1994 version.

ISO 9001:2000 is used for registration purposes and it defines the minimum requirements needed to achieve customer satisfaction. Although ISO 9004:2000 may not be used for registration, it's recommended that managers who wish to move beyond the basic requirements of ISO 9001:2000 use ISO 9004:2000 as a guide in their pursuit of a more robust quality management system.

What is the purpose of ISO 9004:2000, and how should it be used?

ISO 9001:2000 and ISO 9004:2000 have been designed to be used together for greater benefits to organizations' complete quality management system. However, the documents can be used independently. ISO 9004:2000 has been developed to provide guidance to management on the application of the quality system. It's also meant to assist organizations that wish to move beyond the minimum requirements of ISO 9001:2000, but it isn't meant as guidance for compliance with ISO 9001:2000. ISO 9004:2000 also contains a self-assessment tool to assist organizations in determining the maturity of their quality management system.

3. RELEASING THE REVISIONS

When will ISO 9001:2000 be released?

It's expected that the final version of ISO 9001:2000 will be published by the International Organization for Standardization (ISO) in the fourth quarter of 2000. However, it could be delayed, depending on how many iterations the standard goes through as well as the results of the voting by the member countries of Technical Committee 176.

I've heard that ISO 9001:2000 has moved to a "DIS" status. What does this mean?

DIS is the abbreviation for Draft International Standard. In this stage of ISO 9001:2000's development process, it's in a draft format and it is expected that no more "significant" changes will be made from now until the time of publication. Typically, the DIS proceeds, with minimal changes, to become a Final Draft International Standard (FDIS) and eventually becomes the published standard. A word of caution: Because there has been considerable discussion and debate from the various TC 176 member countries during the revision process, there is a possibility that more changes will take place between the DIS and the FDIS. It is the authors' opinion that the main components of the DIS will remain unchanged. The DIS is currently available to the public. Copies may be ordered from the American Society for Quality *(see section 7 of this chapter, Other Information)*.

In which languages will ISO 9001:2000 be available?
    ISO 9001:2000 will be published in three official languages: English, French, and Russian.

Once ISO 9001:2000 is published, will my organization have to change our quality management system's documentation structure?
    No. You will not have to change your structure; however, you will have to incorporate the new requirements into your quality management system in the relevant areas. It's a good idea to review a copy of the draft standard to get an idea of what the new structure looks like. This will give you a head start on making the necessary updates.

4. REGISTRATION CONCERNS

If my organization is currently registered to ISO 9002:1994, how will the revised standard affect our registration?
    Accredited certificates issued to ISO 9001/9002/9003:1994 will expire three years from the date of ISO 9001:2000's publication. If you currently hold an ISO 9002 certificate, you can still explain the reduction of scope within your quality manual as previously done for such elements as 4.4 Design Control. Also, if you are already certified, your registrar will most likely contact you with its timing requirements for updating to ISO 9001:2000.

If my organization is planning on registering to ISO 9001:1994 or ISO 9002:1994 within the next year, how will the release of the revised standard affect our efforts?
    If you have not already done so, select a registrar and explain your situation as soon as possible. At some point after the final publication of ISO 9001:2000, registrars will not be able to perform certification audits to the 1994 version. Your registrar will be able to provide information on when it will require compliance to ISO 9001:2000.

My organization is thinking about developing and implementing an ISO 9001 quality management system. We have not yet decided if we will pursue registration. Should we wait until the revised standard is released?

There is no need to wait until the new standard is officially published. The DIS is currently available to the public. This document's content is very close to that of the final standard. Most companies need 18–24 months to completely implement a full quality management system. By the time a registration audit would be initiated, the final standard would likely already be published, and the organization could easily make any necessary modifications to ensure compliance.

What if my organization chooses to keep our system compliant to the 1994 version? Will we be able to remain certified?

No. The 1994 version will remain in effect for up to three years from the date the final standard is released. This time frame is dependent on your registrar's requirements and, potentially, your surveillance audit schedule. After this established time frame, if your system is not updated, it will be considered noncompliant.

I work for an ISO 9002 registered company. How will we be able to tell the difference between companies with design responsibilities and those without design responsibilities now that the standard only reflects ISO 9001?

Certification/registration bodies will need to take particular care in defining the scope of the certificates issued. This will require very clear and concise descriptions of the activities of an organization that are to be included in the registration process.

Will it be possible to register my organization's quality system to the ISO 9004:2000 document?

No. ISO 9004:2000 is a guidance document only and is not intended for certification purposes.

Once ISO 9001:2000 is released, will a full reassessment of my organization be required?

This is primarily a decision to be made between your organization and your registrar. Accreditation bodies worldwide will be providing guidance for the numerous certification bodies on how to proceed regarding this issue. ISO TC 176 is working with the International Accreditation Forum to provide relevant and timely information.

Will I need to rewrite all of my documentation to comply with the process model approach?

Every organization should carefully think through how it will approach the revisions. If the current documentation has been written well and is compliant, there should not be a need to rewrite all of the documentation. The organization will need to review the revisions against its current documentation in order to determine the changes needed.

5. AUDITING ISSUES

Will we need to retrain our internal auditors?

Yes. You will need to train your internal auditors on the structure, content, and terminology of the revised standard. The auditors will need to understand the process management concept and will need to develop auditing checklists that cover the processes within your organization as they relate to ISO 9001:2000's requirements.

Will third-party auditors need to be retrained?

Yes. The third-party auditors will also receive adequate training prior to the release of ISO 9001:2000. Many registrars will base their auditor training programs on the DIS document. Contact your registrar to find out when its auditors will receive training.

Third-party auditors will need to audit your organization using a process-oriented approach. Rather than focusing on the ISO 9001 requirements within a particular function, they will focus on entire business processes across the organization. They will need to determine how those business processes and the associated documentation meet the ISO 9001:2000 requirements.

Has a common auditing standard for ISO 9001 and ISO 14001 been developed?

At the present time, ISO 10011, the common guideline document for auditing, is being consolidated with ISO 14010, ISO 14011, and ISO 14012. The planned publication date for this new document (ISO 19011) is in the second quarter of 2001. Keep in mind that this is a guidance document providing a foundation for structuring the audit system. Because it won't be released with ISO 9001:2000, the current versions of the audit guidelines for the ISO 9000 family and ISO 14000 family can still be used.

6. SERVICE AND SMALL ORGANIZATIONS

Will small organizations still be able to adapt the requirements of the standard to fit their needs?

From the very beginning, one of the intents behind ISO 9001 was that the standard be generic enough to adapt to any organization, small or large, manufacturing or service. This intent has not changed. As in the past, it will be up to the individual organization to determine the level of complexity needed to meet its organizational and customer needs.

Will the "Guide for Small Businesses" be updated?

At the present time, the guide is expected to become a brochure issued by ISO.

My organization provides services. Will the revised standard apply to us?

ISO 9001:2000 is intended to apply to all types of organizations, including those in the service industry. The standard is written in generic terms and is adaptable to small, medium, and large organizations.

7. OTHER INFORMATION

If I want to know more about the revised standards, where can I get the information?

There are a number of sources from which to get information:

■ American Society for Quality (ASQ)—(800) 248-1946 or *www.asq.org*
■ Registrar Accreditation Board (RAB)—(888) 722-2440 or *www.rabnet.com*
■ U.S. Standards Group—*standardsgroup.asq.org*

The DIS versions are published as a set (including ISO 9000, ISO 9001, and ISO 9004) and can be ordered from ASQ. The ISO/TC 176/SC2 Web site, *www.bsi.org.uk/iso-176-sc2,* contains detailed information on the revisions and is updated regularly. Information can also be obtained from ISO's Web site at *www.iso.ch.*

You may also contact the authors of this book:
Jeanne Ketola, CEO
Pathway Consulting Inc.
Telephone: (612) 473-1702 or (800) 553-2766
Fax: (612) 473-1733
E-mail: *pathtrack@aol.com*

Kathy Roberts, President
Sunrise Consulting Inc.
Telephone: (919) 961-7951
Fax: (919) 782-7614
E-mail: *thesunrise@mindspring.com*

Appendix 1

Record Requirements

T he chart on the following page shows the records required for ISO 9001:2000. Keep in mind that most records need to demonstrate results and any follow-up actions taken. ISO 9001:2000 explicitly requires that records be controlled.

Organizations should also carefully review ISO 9001:2000 for required documentation that is not considered a record or a procedure. This includes items such as the quality policy, the quality manual, and planning of realization processes.

ISO 9001:2000 Record Requirements by Section

Section		Description
5.4.2	Quality planning	Results of quality planning
5.6.3	Review output	Management review results
6.2.2	Training, awareness, and competency	Education, experience, training, and qualification records
7.1	Planning of realization processes	Provide confidence of process and product conformity
7.2.2	Review of product requirements	Contract review and follow-up actions
7.3.4	Design and/or development review	Results of the review and follow-up actions
7.3.5	Design and/or development verification	Verification results and follow-up actions
7.3.6	Design and/or development validation	Validation results and follow-up actions
7.3.7	Control of design and/or development validation	Results of review of changes and follow-up actions
7.4.1	Purchasing control	Supplier evaluations and follow-up actions
7.5.2	Identification and traceability	Unique identification of product
7.5.3	Customer property	Reporting of customer property lost, damaged, or unsuitable for use
7.5.5	Validation of processes	Validation requirements for records
7.6	Control of measuring and monitoring devices	(a) Where no standards exist, basis used for calibration
7.6	Control of measuring and monitoring devices	(b) Results of calibration
8.2.2	Internal audit	Results of internal audits
8.2.2	Internal audit	Verification of implementation of corrective action through follow-up activities
8.5.2	Corrective action	Corrective action results taken
8.5.3	Preventive action	Preventive action results taken

Appendix 2

Clause-to-Section Cross-Reference Matrix

The chart on the following pages compares ISO 9001:1994's clauses to ISO 9001:2000's sections. 1994's 20 clauses are shown across the top of the matrix. ISO 9001:2000's sections 4–8 are listed down the left side of the matrix.

ISO 9001:1994's 20 clauses are:

4.1   Management Responsibility
4.2   Quality System
4.3   Contract Review
4.4   Design Control
4.5   Document and Data Control
4.6   Purchasing
4.7   Control of Customer-Supplied Product
4.8   Product Identification and Traceability
4.9   Process Control
4.10   Inspection and Testing
4.11   Control of Inspection, Measuring, and Test Equipment
4.12   Inspection and Test Status
4.13   Control of Nonconforming Product
4.14   Corrective and Preventive Action
4.15   Handling, Storage, Packaging, Preservation, and Delivery
4.16   Control of Quality Records
4.17   Internal Quality Audits
4.18   Training
4.19   Servicing
4.20   Statistical Techniques

| ISO 9001:1994 Clauses (Across) → | 4.1 | 4.2 | 4.3 | 4.4 | 4.5 | 4.6 | 4.7 | 4.8 | 4.9 | 4.10 | 4.11 | 4.12 | 4.13 | 4.14 | 4.15 | 4.16 | 4.17 | 4.18 | 4.19 | 4.20 |
ISO 9001:2000 Sections (Down) ↓																				
4 Quality management system		■																		
4.1 General requirements		■																		
4.2 General documentation requirements	■	■																		
5 Management responsibility																				
5.1 Management commitment	■																			
5.2 Customer focus	■		■																	
5.3 Quality policy	■																			
5.4 Planning																				
5.4.1 Quality objectives		■																		
5.4.2 Quality planning		■																		
5.5 Administration																				
5.5.1 General																				
5.5.2 Responsibility and authority	■																			
5.5.3 Management representative	■																			
5.5.4 Internal communication		■																		
5.5.5 Quality manual																				
5.5.6 Control of documents					■															
5.5.7 Control of quality records																■				
5.6 Management review																				
5.6.1 General	■																			
5.6.2 Review input													■	■						
5.6.3 Review output																■	■			
6 Resource management																				
6.1 Provision of resources	■																			
6.2 Human resources																				
6.2.1 Assignment of personnel																				
6.2.2 Training, awareness and competency																		■		
6.3 Facilities									■											
6.4 Work Environment									■											

ISO 9001:1994 Clauses (Across) ISO 9001:2000 Sections (Down)	4.1	4.2	4.3	4.4	4.5	4.6	4.7	4.8	4.9	4.10	4.11	4.12	4.13	4.14	4.15	4.16	4.17	4.18	4.19	4.20
7 Product realization																				
7.1 Planning of realization processes		■								■						■				
7.2 Customer-related processes																				
7.2.1 Identification of customer requirements			■																	
7.2.2 Review of product requirements			■																	
7.2.3 Customer communication																				
7.3 Design and/or development																				
7.3.1 Design and/or development planning				■																
7.3.2 Design and/or development inputs				■																
7.3.3 Design and/or development outputs				■																
7.3.4 Design and/or development review				■																
7.3.5 Design and/or development verification				■												■				
7.3.6 Design and/or development validation				■																
7.3.7 Control of design and/or development changes				■																
7.4 Purchasing																				
7.4.1 Purchasing control						■														
7.4.2 Purchasing information						■														
7.4.3 Verification of purchased product							■													
7.5 Production and service operations																				
7.5.1 Operations control									■						■	■			■	
7.5.2 Identification and traceability								■				■				■				
7.5.3 Customer property							■													
7.5.4 Preservation of product															■					
7.5.5 Validation of processes									■							■				
7.6 Control of measuring and monitoring devices											■									
8 Measurement, analysis and improvement																				
8.1 Planning																				
8.2 Measurement and monitoring																				
8.2.1 Customer satisfaction																				
8.2.2 Internal audit																	■			
8.2.3 Measurement and monitoring of processes																				
8.2.4 Measurement and monitoring of product										■		■					■			■
8.3 Control of nonconformity													■							
8.4 Analysis of data														■						■
8.5 Improvement																				
8.5.1 Planning for continual improvement	■																			
8.5.2 Corrective Action														■						
8.5.3 Preventive Action														■						

About the Authors

Jeanne Ketola, CEO of Pathway Consulting Inc., has more than 20 years of business experience in a diverse range of industries. She has a bachelor's degree in business management and is an ASQ Certified Quality Auditor, an RAB Quality Systems Auditor, and a trained management coach. Ketola is actively involved in the U.S. TAG to TC 176, which is instrumental in reviewing and writing the ISO 9000 revisions, establishing all U.S. positions, and voting on the final draft standard prior to publication. She has participated at a national level in writing the auditing guidelines for ISO 9000-Q10011. Ketola is the secretary of the ANSI Z1 Executive Committee, which is responsible for all actions relating to national quality standards.

Jeanne Ketola, CEO
Pathway Consulting Inc.
Telephone: (612) 473-1702 or (800) 553-2766
Fax: (612) 473-1733
E-mail: *pathtrack@aol.com*

Kathy Roberts, President of Sunrise Consulting Inc., has held various quality engineering and quality management positions in a diverse range of industries during the past 10 years. She has a bachelor's degree in industrial engineering and is an ASQ Certified Quality Auditor and a trained examiner for the North Carolina Performance Excellence Process. Roberts is an active member of the U.S. TAG to TC 176 and is the vice chair of the ANSI Z1 Executive Committee.

Kathy Roberts, President
Sunrise Consulting Inc.
Telephone: (919) 961-7951
Fax: (919) 782-7614
E-mail: *thesunrise@mindspring.com*

Index

Sections & Clauses